A
WILDERNESS
OF
WATER

based on true events

BEN ROBICHEAU

A Wilderness of Water
© 2023 Ben Robicheau

Cover image: Rebekah Wetmore
Editor: Andrew Wetmore

ISBN: 978-1-990187-90-2
First edition June, 2023

MOOSE HOUSE
PUBLICATIONS

2475 Perotte Road
Annapolis County, NS
B0S 1A0

moosehousepress.com
info@moosehousepress.com

We live and work in Mi'kma'ki, the ancestral and unceded territory of the Mi'kmaw People. This territory is covered by the "Treaties of Peace and Friendship" which Mi'kmaw and Wolastoqiyik (Maliseet) People first signed with the British Crown in 1725. The treaties did not deal with surrender of lands and resources but in fact recognized Mi'kmaq and Wolastoqiyik (Maliseet) title and established the rules for what was to be an ongoing relationship between nations. We are all Treaty people.

Also by Ben Robicheau

and available from Moose House Publications

Fish and Dicks: Case files from the Digby Neck & Islands Fish-Gutting Service & Detective Agency (with Jim Prime)

Two Ferries Out: growing up on Brier Island

Long Trip

The sea is a wilderness of waves,
A desert of water.
We dip and dive,
Rise and roll,
Hide and are hidden
On the sea.
Day, night,
Night, day,
The sea is a desert of waves,
A wilderness of water.

—Langston Hughes

This book is based on two separate but connected tragic events that took place in the Bay of Fundy area in 1958 and 1963. Much of the details are, of necessity, fictional, but the core of the story is drawn from official police records and the personal experience and testimony of those who lived through the event.

With the permission of the families involved, I am using the real names of the central characters. Of the rest, some of the names and characters are real; some of them are made up. None of the words or actions are meant to be representative of any specific person.

The factual information in this story comes from the official records of the Yarmouth and Digby RCMP detachments and the documentation of events recorded by Fannie Welch-Urquhart in *A Family's Life on Peters Island Lighthouse Station & Westport, Brier Island, Nova Scotia*; and in *The Search: Missing Person, David Gordon Welch*; as well as from the memories of my father, Raymond Robicheau, of myself as a fifteen-year-old boy, and of others who were involved at the time.

The conversations that take place in this story are entirely the invention of the author, but based on personal knowledge of the place and its people, and on his own impressions and memories of the events at the time.

Ben Robicheau
May, 2023

In Memory of
brothers David and Gerald Welch
and their cousin
Donald McDormand

And also of the far too many Long and Brier Islanders who for generations have gone down to the sea, only to disappear forever into that wilderness of water.

Southwestern Nova Scotia

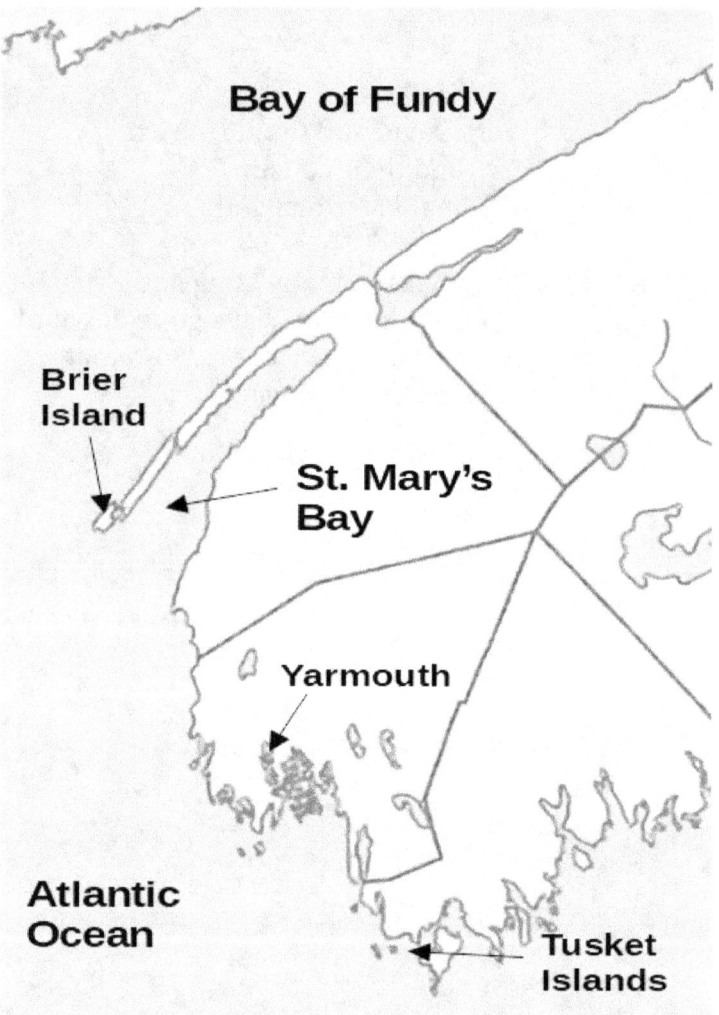

Bay of Fundy

Brier Island

St. Mary's Bay

Yarmouth

Atlantic Ocean

Tusket Islands

A Wilderness of Water

Images from the Welch family collection

1: The dull-yellow light

Thursday, December 19, 1963

Where is that damned high-flyer?

In frustration, Donald McDormand let go of the wheel and took a few seconds to stretch and arch his back. Then he shook his whole body, rotated his neck and shoulders, and stood on one leg, then the other, giving the opposite leg a vigorous shake each time. He was trying to 'get the blood flowing again.'

Donald had been standing at the wheel of his fishing boat, *Ruth Lillian II,* for over eight hours now, fighting fatigue, muscle-ache, and, for the last few of those hours, the ever-increasing wind and waves. His body was starting to rebel on him, seizing up in response to the tediousness and tenseness of the situation, and his aching eyes were rebelling, too. He squeezed them shut for a moment, gave them a rub, and then slowly reopened them.

That gave him no relief at all. After all the hours of straining to see through a salt-covered wheelhouse window into the pitch-black night, his eyeballs felt like they'd been rolled in sand.

The long hours on his feet and the continuous need to adjust to the bucking and rolling of the boat were taking a toll on his back. He stretched again, trying to loosen things up.

Donald had just turned twenty-two a couple of months ago. He considered himself to be in pretty good shape, but lately was starting to feel like an old man.

Of course, this was the third night in a row that they'd come out here on the Southwest Ledge, setting trawl a dozen miles from land. And then, as if fishing all night wasn't hard enough, on the last two mornings, as soon as they'd gotten in from their all-nighter, he and Gerald had turned right around and gone back out again to spend the rest of the day trying their luck out back of the island.

Over the last three days they had only had a couple of decent meals and had not managed to grab more than a dozen hours of sleep between the two of them. And what sleep they did get was mostly just a few minutes at a time here and there, not really enough rest to restore the energy required for a job like this.

Donald guessed that the shortage of food and sleep probably had something to do with the lousy way he was feeling right now. *Ah, well.*

This storm that he had been fighting the last few hours was rapidly coming down on them now, and it looked like it was shaping up to be a nasty one. That was why they were working non-stop, trying to get in as much fishing as possible before the bad weather hit.

Once they got this trawl hauled, they'd head for home, and that would most likely be it for the next few days. It'd be a while before the weather let them get back out here again, and until then, they'd have plenty of time to rest up.

The windshield wiper, salvaged from a wrecked pick-up truck and bolted to the top of the window frame, struggled spasmodically back and forth, doing a valiant, but ultimately futile, job of scraping the glass clear of wind-plastered snow and half-frozen sea spray. Straining his aching eyes to squint out between smeary, half-dried streaks of salt-water slush in search of a dim little light that should be bobbing around out there in that vast sea of darkness, Donald was just about ready to give up.

This was their second attempt to find that one last marker buoy. Conditions had been a lot better a few hours earlier, when they had managed to pick up the first trawl lines without much trouble. They'd got a pretty good haul of fish off of them, too, mostly haddock, but also cod, and even the odd pollock.

But while they worked, the weather had grown steadily worse, and now, in their second attempt to relocate that spot where they had set their final line of trawl, they were dealing with not just the poor visibility one would normally expect out on the open ocean on such a starless night, but also the thick, wet snow, high seas, and punishing winds of a rapidly-intensifying winter storm.

On their first go-round at picking up this final trawl marker, Gerald Welch, the only other crew member and Donald's cousin, younger by one year, had been the one who spotted the faint glow of the battery-operated light through the darkness and driving snow. They had been relieved to finally locate the high-flyer, a wooden keg with an upright six-foot bamboo pole protruding from it.

From the top of the pole fluttered a home-made triangular flag which Donald had cut from an old oilskin coat and painted in his signature colours, the same colours he used to mark his lobster buoys. The flag wasn't much use at night, so just beneath it sat the battery-operated light and, below that, a metal radar reflector.

The reflector wasn't of much help to them, either, since the *Ruth Lillian II* was not equipped with radar, a situation Donald hoped to rectify as soon as he got the boat all paid off. For now, the reflector warned off other, better-equipped vessels and kept them from running down their fishing gear in thick fog, or in the darkness of night, or in a storm like this.

Right now, at five o'clock in the morning, all they had to help locate and identify their trawl-line in this pitch-blackness was that elusive little pale-yellow light.

Donald hoped they did better this time around. The first attempt at picking up this trawl hadn't gone so well.

When Gerald had finally located the marker, Donald had nudged up the throttle control a touch and nosed the *Ruth Lillian II* around a little more to put her more bow-first into the wind. Approaching the buoy, he spun the wheel, gave the engine another little shot of full throttle, and then quickly pulled it back down to an idle, kicking the stern sideways a bit to get in a little closer to the high-flyer and, he hoped, giving his cousin a better chance at hooking the line fastened to the bottom of the buoy.

Then, just as Gerald reached out with the long-handled gaff to snag the rope, a large roller caught the boat, lifting it up and away and simultaneously dropping the high-flyer down into the trough of the same wave. The boat slued sideways off the wave, Gerald missed hooking the line, and, in trying to avoid getting swamped by one of those big-assed waves they were dealing with now, they'd managed to get themselves all turned around in the dark. They'd lost their bearings on that light and had now spent the best part of the last thirty minutes trying to spot it again.

Gerald was standing five feet behind Donald in the partial protection of the wheelhouse awning, just at the edge of the open aft part of the boat, peering out into the darkness. He was clad in well-worn, dark-green oilskin pants and jacket, black rubber boots, and once-white mittens. The home-made mittens couldn't do much to keep his hands dry, but the thick, double-knit wool kept his fingers warm enough that he could still keep a good grip when he needed to.

He held the gaff loosely in his right hand and his left forearm was up across his face, trying, with limited success, to shield his slitted eyes from the salt spray and freezing snow that was rapidly turning into little bullets of sleet as it pelted in off the water with stinging force.

Once again, he was the one to catch a glimpse of the dull-yellow light bobbing ahead of them and off to the starboard. He shouted to Donald and pointed. "There it is! Over there to the right!"

"I see the son of a bitch!"

Donald spun the wheel and gave the engine a quick shot of gas, kicking the boat around to line up for a run at the buoy. Then, as he neared the buoy, he throttled back; he'd make his approach a little more cautiously this time.

This was going to be their last chance to snag it: the weather was going all-to-shit real fast. As much as he hated to do it, if they couldn't retrieve their gear this time around, he'd have to seriously consider abandoning it and whatever fish it had caught, and making for home.

Truth to tell, he grudgingly admitted to himself, *we should have been well on our way back to Brier Island long before this*.

Donald tried to keep track of the wildly-dancing smudge of light, watching it intermittently appear and disappear behind the waves as both the boat and the buoy rose and fell. He was closing in on the high-flyer from the weather side, hoping to give Gerald on the lee side of the boat what little protection he could from the storm.

Keeping an eye on the chaotic wave action, he attempted, as best as he could, to maneuver so that both boat and buoy would be more or less rising and falling together.

He edged in a little closer, and Gerald, watching his chance, again leaned out over the rail, reached out with his gaff, and this time successfully snagged the rope.

He rapidly pulled it to the side of the boat and, with a cry of triumph, deftly manhandled the keg and its trailing anchor line over the rail.

The trawl line, the line that actually does the fishing, is attached to the anchor rope about one fathom, or six feet, from the bottom. It then runs along horizontally just above the ocean floor for about a third of a mile, or half a kilometre or so, where it is secured to another anchor and buoy line.

Gerald quickly untied this end of the trawl line and took one and a half turns around the wooden capstan of the hauler. Running off a power-take-off attachment on the front of the boat engine, the hauler took some of the need for brute strength out of hauling the trawl aboard; but not all of it by any means. A lot of physical effort was still required.

Gerald slipped a pair of 'nippers'—red rubber bands that protected his hands and helped him get a better grip on the line—on over his mittens, grabbed the end of the line where it came off the capstan, and began to slowly pull in the long trawl with its burden of fish.

Gonna be another good night, Donald thought, his aches and pains forgotten for the moment as the first hook appeared and the first of many silvery haddock flopped, flipping and thrashing, over the rail, only to be flung unceremoniously into the already-nearly-full fish box.

Maybe he had taken a bit of a risk after all, ignoring his father's warnings and heading out in this bad weather. He had to admit that, as it turned out, it was not the best time to be here right now, almost two hours out, in this grey area where the Bay of Fundy and the Atlantic Ocean meet.

They needed to start back soon, but it looked like taking this bit of a chance had paid off. He would be going home with a more-than-decent haul of fish.

I guess this will show the old man, Donald thought with satisfaction.

2: Fish while the fishin's good

The previous day

Just about ten hours earlier, Donald had been at home in Westport, in the old house near the ferry wharf that his parents had inherited just a year previously from his grandfather, William McDormand—known by one and all as Billy Mac.

Donald was sitting at the kitchen table with his mother, Eileen, and his father, Bernard, better known by his boyhood nickname of Ace, engaging in what had grown over the last couple of hours to become a rather intense disagreement between the two men.

Pushing aside his half-empty supper plate, Ace planted both elbows on the table and leaned forward, as if hoping that closer proximity might more firmly impress his words upon his son. "I'm tellin' ya, Donald, only a fool would think of goin' offshore tonight with that nor'easter on the way. It's going to get damn dirty out there!"

"Take it easy, old man! They're saying that storm ain't even supposed to hit until well after daylight.

We'll be back home long before it amounts to anything."

"Don't be a damn fool! You know you can't take what that marine weather report says as gospel. People call it 'The Probs' because they use that word in every radio report: probability of this, probability of that. They know better than to claim they can predict the weather one hundred percent, and you should damn-well know better than to rely on their report one hundred percent!"

"We're not goin' all that far. The Southwest Ledge ain't more'n ten miles out. If it starts lookin' real bad, we can be back home inside of a couple hours. We had a good haul last night and we oughtta be able to do the same tonight. Once that storm hits, fishin'll be done for a few days. We won't be able to get out again 'til it all calms down some, and the weather this time of year is bad enough anyway, so who knows when it'll be fit to leave the harbour again. You know what they say, you gotta fish while the fishin's good."

"You can't count on how those winter storms are gonna behave when they hit open water," Ace replied. "Sometimes they just stall and hang around for days at a time, other times they speed up and breed gales that are way stronger than what the forecast was callin' for. I been fishin' these waters since before you were even thought of, and I tell you, boy, I wouldn't take a chance on goin' out in weather like this."

Donald motioned toward the living room window overlooking the harbour, where Grand Passage, dividing Brier Island from neighbouring Long Island, presented the appearance of nothing more threatening than a mill pond. The harbour, at the moment, was what the locals referred to as flat-ass ca'm; the village lights of Freeport across the water were reflecting off the mirror-like surface in jagged streaks.

"Looks pretty good out there right now!"

"You know that don't mean shit! The weather around these islands can change from one minute to the next. And what's happenin' inside the harbour now don't have nothin' at all to do what might be goin' on outside later on."

Ace, a fisherman for well over forty of his sixty-two years, was born and had lived his entire life on Brier Island. He was therefore no stranger to the havoc that could be wreaked by the sudden shift of wind and tide that was so common around these two islands at the end of Digby Neck.

Surrounded by the record-setting Bay of Fundy tides on one side, the strong ebb and flow of St. Mary's Bay on the other, with the vast might of the whole Atlantic Ocean at its back, this was a place of strong and unpredictable currents, as well as dangerous reefs, ledges, and shoals. Located in an area famous for its abundance of lobster, scallops, and herring, as well as a wide variety of commercially-valuable fish, and touching on highly-trafficked international shipping routes, it was no surprise that over the years the waters around the islands had become littered with dozens of wrecks, earning this area the title "Graveyard of the Fundy".

For over three hundred years—beginning back in the early days of sail and continuing on to the age of steam and up to the present-day of modern radar and GPS equipped vessels—rocks and reefs, accidents, tides, and storms have continued to claim a heavy toll, leaving a legacy of loss and grief that serves as a dire warning for the less-fortunate or less-attentive sailor.

The waters around these islands were long-ago found, through unfortunate experience by early mariners, to be so notoriously treacherous that the Nova Scotia government selected Brier Island as the site of one of the first lighthouses the province built. Completed in 1809 on the most south-westerly point of the most south-westerly piece of land in the province, Western Light, on Whipple's Point, was expected to be such a benefit to the safety of commercial sea traffic travelling up and down the Maritime coast that the neighbouring New Brunswick government voluntarily paid half the cost of construction and continued to contribute to its upkeep for the next several years.

Unfortunately, by 1818 this first lighthouse was being described as "So vilely constructed and ill lighted" that it was deemed to be more of a hazard to passing sailors than it was a help. By 1832 it had been replaced by an octagonal wooden tower with a metal lantern. A large fog signal building also stood on the site.

This tower burned down in 1944 and was re-placed by the non-flammable concrete structure that stands today. Eventually this small island would come to have three lighthouses, one for every mile of its length.

Despite this unusually dense concentration of lighthouses, tragedy continued, and still continues, to be a frequent visitor to the doorsteps of island residents. There is scarcely a household on either is-land that has not been touched at some time by a loss at sea.

Ace sat back in his chair in exasperation. He could see that, in this case, his years of experience and knowledge were going to be no match for the enthu-siasm and arrogance of youth. Donald, just turned twenty-two in October, had only six months earlier become the proud owner of his own boat.

Except, in his mind he wasn't quite the owner yet, not until it was paid off. Donald had acquired the *Ruth Lillian II* in the way that many young island men became boat owners: with a bit of financial help from someone else.

The usual source of credit, the banks, were not overly eager to lend money to young men with no financial history, no record or prospects of a steady income, and no collateral except a second-hand fishing boat. After several years of learning the trade while fishing with his father, Donald felt he was ready to be captain of his own ship, so when a boat came up for sale across the harbour in Freeport, he approached Raymond Robicheau, local fish-buyer and store owner, for help with financing.

The *Ruth Lillian II* looked to be a good buy. She was a Cape Island style boat, built specifically for the conditions and methods of fishing in this end of the province: she was forty-two feet in length, thirteen feet, two inches, in width, only five years old, and had been well taken care of.

A second-hand Chevy car engine that had already put in many a highway mile provided her power, but many of the boats in the harbour were similarly equipped, so that was not a concern. Most of these old, salvaged engines took well to their second life at sea and the fishermen gave not a second thought to their reliability as they travelled far off-shore in every kind of weather.

A deal was soon reached and Raymond 'backed a note' with the bank to buy the boat. The handshake agreement between the two men was that Donald would deliver all the fish he caught to Raymond's fish plant at the going market price, where a 'boat share' would be deducted from each payout until the *Ruth Lillian II* was paid off. Then the title would be transferred over to Donald and he would finally own the boat, free and clear.

This was a time-honoured system that worked well for both parties. Fish processors were guaranteed a steady source of supply, and young fishermen looking to set out on their own gained access to a boat and equipment they might not have otherwise been able to afford. It was the way things had long been done on the island, and Donald had no problem taking advantage of it; but the sooner the boat was paid off, the better, as far as he was concerned.

And fishing was good right now. The price of haddock had recently risen from seven to eight cents a pound, so he was, by God, going to take advantage of it, even if there might be a bit of risk involved.

Donald's cousin Gerald had his own reasons for taking a chance on the weather. Just turned twenty-one two days ago, and a recently married man, he felt a husband's responsibility to provide for Carolyn, his new bride; plus, it was the eighteenth of December, one week to Christmas. Only a fool would turn down the chance to make a little extra money at this time of year.

But the major reason Gerald had jumped at the chance, when Donald asked if he wanted to put in a few days of haulin' trawl, was the opportunity to add to his nest egg. Early in the new year, he and Carolyn were planning to head out west in search of work and a new life. A few days of fishing would add a little more heft to the bankroll that was going to finance their future.

The wooden kitchen chair creaked in protest as Ace tipped it back on its hind legs and pulled a package of 'makin's' and some rolling papers from his shirt pocket. As he slowly built himself a cigarette, he glanced over at his wife, hoping for a little support in the discussion with their son.

So far, Eileen hadn't said more than a couple of words on the subject. He could tell that she was concerned, but he could also see that she thought this was a discussion better left to the men.

His cigarette complete, Ace scratched a wooden kitchen match across the tabletop and held it to its twisted end. As the paper flared up and immediately diminished to a glowing ember, he planted all four chair-legs back on the floor with a thud, took a long drag off the cigarette, and, eyeing his son across the table, slowly exhaled the smoke out through his nose in a lazy blue cloud that curled slowly up around his head.

Resigning himself to a reluctant decision, he made his final statement on the subject. "Well, I can see you boys got your own reasons for pushin' your luck. I guess nothin' I got to say is going to make any difference. I only hope you use the good judgment God gave ya out there."

3: Just taking a minute

If it was up to me, Ada Welch thought to herself, *I'd leave him right there.*

Ada was standing in the kitchen doorway of the Western Light lightkeeper's house. She was looking at her son sprawled out on the living room sofa, fast asleep.

Gerald was the baby of the family, the youngest of six, three girls and three boys. She had been pleasantly surprised when he had shown up at her door here at Whipple's Point about forty minutes earlier, taking advantage of a little down-time to visit his parents before he and Donald had to set out for the night.

Percy and Ada Welch had been lighthouse keepers for over thirty years. They were called 'wickies' back in the days when Percy got his first light.

As a teenager during World War I, Percy had joined the Navy. After returning home in 1923, he tried his hand at fishing. Finding the fishing trade to be less than lucrative, he supplemented it with a brief foray into rum-running; a venture that came to an abrupt end when his father found out about it.

To try to make up for this lapse in judgment and to get back into his father's good graces, Percy switched sides and joined the Rum Chaser Fleet for a time. In 1927 he married Ada McDormand and soon after reached the decision that the life of a fisherman was not for him.

In 1929, Percy found what was to become his life-long vocation, when he and Ada and their first-born, Freda, moved to Peters Island as "Keepers of the Light".

Figure 1: Peters Island

They spent the next eleven years and raised a family there, the only inhabitants—except for a few cows and sheep and a lot of seagulls—of the tiny speck of rock and grass that splits the southern entrance to the passage between Long and Brier Islands. Eventually, as their family continued to increase, the remote location proved too difficult to deal with.

Just how difficult and downright dangerous it could get was brought home to them in dramatic fashion one October evening, when Ada went into labour with Fannie, their fourth child and the last one to be born while they were still living on Peters Island.

They were lucky that Ada's cousin and good friend, Dot Welch, was visiting when the labour pains hit. Dot had graduated from the Yarmouth Hospital with a degree in nursing just two weeks before, and proved invaluable in helping transport Ada across the passage to Brier Island.

The first step was to get Ada down to the beach and into a dory, then row her out to Percy's boat, which was anchored just offshore, then transfer Ada from the dory to the boat.

Despite being less than happy about this situation, Ada managed to do it, and was relieved to be on her way to Westport.

Then the single-cylinder make-and-break engine

in Percy's boat quit, leaving them adrift in the dark, in the middle of the harbour.

Using matches to provide the light to examine the oil-soaked engine, Percy ignored Dot's "Good Lord, Perce, you're going to blow us out of the water!" and eventually managed to restart the engine and get them to Billy Mac's, Ada's father's, house, just in time.

Before she gave birth to their next child, David, Ada and Percy decided it was probably a good idea for all involved if they relocated with their four kids to a house on Brier Island, with Percy continuing to travel back and forth to spend his shifts on Peters Island by himself.

Over the ensuing years two more children joined the family and Percy would go on to serve at all three of the island lighthouses. After he moved up to Northern Light for a period, his station for the last few years had been as head lightkeeper at Western Light on Whipple's Point.

Now, standing here in this doorway, watching her son sleep, Ada thought back to Gerald's wedding day, just two months earlier, when a small group of friends and family had gathered to see him and Carolyn get married in this very living room.

Wouldn't you know it, just as Reverend Derby was about to start the ceremony, the fog had started to roll in. For a few moments Percy found himself in conflict: should he delay the ceremony while he went to start up the foghorn, or should he just slip out quietly and miss his chance to see his son get married?

He was saved from having to decide by one of the assistant lightkeepers. Wickerson Lent sprung into action and quickly fired up the big engine that powered the air compressor. Soon the assembled guests were experiencing the conversation-stopping, dish-rattling, deep-throated double blast that was the distinctive sound of one of the most powerful foghorns on the whole East Coast.

Thanks to Wick's quick action, the wedding was able to get started right on schedule, but it ran on a bit longer than expected. Ada smiled to herself as she remembered Reverend Derby nervously keeping an eye on his watch and pausing after every few lines of his marriage sermon to allow for the next scheduled bellow of the foghorn.

However brief this visit today may be, and despite the fact that he was sleeping through most of it, she was thankful that Gerald had found the time to stop by. Since his marriage, he had been living over on Long Island with Carolyn's parents, the Howards; that, and the fact that the moderate climate on Brier Island created a winter-long freeze-thaw cycle that often made the dirt road to Western Light impassible with drifts of snow one day and deep, muddy ruts the next, meant visits to this remote part of the island were sometimes few and far between. She hadn't even got to see him on his twenty-first birthday, just two days earlier.

Immediately upon Gerald's arrival, Ada had set to making him something to eat while he took the opportunity to stretch out on the couch "just for a few minutes."

She hated to wake him now, when he was sleeping so soundly. He needed the rest. He and Donald had been out for all of last night, and now they were gearing up to go out again tonight with nothing more than an hour or two of sleep...if they were even able to get that much rest in those uncomfortable bunks aboard that damn boat.

Yes, she certainly would have been more than happy to leave him right where he was, not only to let him catch up on his much-needed sleep, but also to keep him safe.

Just four years earlier, Gerald's older brother, David, second-youngest in the family, had disappeared on a night-time trip across the Bay of Fundy. Already the owner of his own boat at the young age of nineteen, David had been making a run across the bay in the lead-up to lobster season to bring back a load of bait from the Grand Manan herring fleet.

Figure 2: David Welch

On this late October trip, David had been storm-stayed for a couple of days with friends in the fishing community of Whitehead on Grand Manan Island when the weather had turned bad on him. Finally, the wind dropped out by dusk of the third day and David took the opportunity to set out in the early evening for the three-hour trip across the bay.

He never arrived home.

The next morning, a Grand Manan fisherman investigating the sound of a racing engine discovered David's boat, the *Elaine D*, run aground on Gull Rock Island, just outside of Whitehead Harbour. The transmission was found to be in gear and the throttle set at cruising speed, but there was no sign of the captain.

Figure 3: David's boat

This sudden disappearance was a devastating blow to David's whole family. The fact that no body was ever recovered created a hole that could never be filled, as well as leaving an air of incompletion.

Not having conclusive evidence of David's demise allowed the nurturing of a faint hope, a possibility that, against all odds, maybe he had somehow survived. This tiny ember of hope would continue to smoulder and flare for years to come.

Ada turned at the sound of her husband coming in through the kitchen door. Percy had been out checking the station's equipment and supplies in preparation for the coming storm.

"Better wake him up, it's getting late. He'll need to get back to town soon."

"I know," Ada replied. "I was just taking a minute."

4: Just another couple of weeks

On his way back to the boat, Gerald pulled his car over in front of the weather-beaten waterside building where their tubs of trawl were being baited.

He walked past a heap of buoys and stacks of coiled rope piled at the side the road, and a few in-need-of-repair lobster traps that were stacked up on the wharf. Several newly-baited tubs of trawl painted in Donald's colours were lined up beside the shop's entry.

Pulling the codline draw-string that lifted the wooden door latch, he entered the poorly-lit fish shop.

A single, fly-specked lightbulb hanging from a fraying cord struggled unsuccessfully to illuminate the shadowy corners of the room. In the centre of the space sat a rusty, old, cast-iron, pot-bellied stove with "Lunenburg Foundry" embossed on the door in raised letters. The heat radiating from it amplified the familiarly-pungent smell of wood smoke, rotting lobster bait, tarred rope, freshly-sawn trap laths, and copper paint that seemed to be common to all these old working fish sheds along the waterfront. A transistor radio sitting among the cobwebs on the cluttered windowsill was tuned to a country and western station.

Along one wall of the room ran a well-worn, rough-lumber workbench, beside which stood a half-baited tub of trawl and a teen-age boy holding a large, wooden-handled knife. Dangling from the edge of a shelf above the bench were several chains of fish hooks.

This was the system baiters used to keep track of how many tubs they had completed. As each tub was finished, another hook was threaded through the eye of the previous hook, adding to the chain for that particular fisherman. On settling-up day—the day the fisherman got paid for the fish they had sold through the week—the hooks were counted and multiplied by a dollar twenty-five, the going rate for baiting the five hundred and thirty-eight hooks on the average trawl, unsnarling any tangled lines, sharpening and straightening bent hooks, and replacing any broken gangens, the short lines that branched off the main line.

"How's it going, Everett?" Gerald greeted the young man at the bench.

"Almost done. Just got to finish up this tub and then one more," Everett Titus replied. As he spoke, he picked a frozen mackerel from the box near his elbow and placed it on the bench. With a few deft strokes of the "chopper" he divided it neatly into three pieces.

"Just cutting up some more bait. The tubs should be at the wharf by nine o'clock."

"Sounds good! See you then."

Normally, the trawl would be baited ahead of time and stored in the freezer over at D. B. Kenny's until it was needed, but he and Donald had run through so many tubs in the last few days that they had no more left in reserve.

Deciding to leave his car where it was, Gerald walked the short distance to the government wharf, better known as "the breakwater", where the *Ruth Lillian II* was tied up. He was feeling pretty good tonight. That short nap and one of his mother's great meals had made him, if not quite a new man, at least a better man than the one he had been a couple of hours ago.

He was glad he had made the time to go see his parents. *It must be hard for them both, now that all their kids are gone.*

The three girls, Freda, Vera, and Fannie, had left years ago to pursue careers and get married. They all lived on the mainland now.

Figure 4: Fannie Welch

Of the boys, Berton was a fisherman over in Free-port. He, Gerald, had spent most of the last year travelling across Canada, and, if things went to plan, would soon be leaving again to head back out west, maybe permanently this time. And then there was David.

It was plain to see what the loss of David had done to his parents, especially his father. Percy wasn't looking too good these days; he had started talking of retirement and was making tentative plans to do some travelling. He'd recently bought a truck, even though he didn't drive; the plan was that Ada would do all the driving on their retirement adventures.

Gerald thought that retirement was probably a good idea for his father. Everyone had been impressed by how Percy had recovered from the stroke he had suf-fered the year after David's disappearance. With a bit of help, he had eventually been able to recover well enough to resume his duties as head lightkeeper. But he hadn't yet been quite able to get back to where he was before the stroke. The past few years had undeniably taken a toll on him; he just wasn't the man he used to be.

And, although she tried her best to keep it to herself, it was obvious that Gerald's mother was far from comfortable with her remaining sons going to sea. He knew that the fact that Berton had recently bought a new boat was upsetting to her. She saw it as confirmation that he wasn't planning on giving up fishing any time soon.

Gerald knew that his mother was not happy with his own return to fishing either—as temporary as it might be—and, to be truthful, he could identify with that feeling.

At the age of sixteen an incident at sea had caused Gerald to reconsider the attractions of life as a fisherman. On a trip across the Bay of Fundy with his brother David in David's newly-acquired boat, an exhaust leak had knocked them both out. It was their uncle Ace and cousin Donald who discovered the *Elaine D* running in circles in the middle of the bay, with the two boys unconscious on the wheelhouse floor.

This experience, plus a couple of other close encounters that David had as the young and inexperienced captain of his own boat, caused Gerald to seriously consider alternatives to a career in fishing.

And after David's disappearance, any remaining lure that a life at sea still held for the seventeen-year-old Gerald had entirely lost its appeal. Soon after, he left the island to join his sister Fannie and her husband, Cyril, in Saint John, New Brunswick, where he found work in a machine shop. After a period of time there, he continued on to take a welding course in Ontario.

Having lived all his life on a small island in the Bay of Fundy, Gerald now found himself nipped by the travel bug and decided to continue his westward trek. The plan was to find work in the big fish canneries of Prince Rupert on the British Columbia coast, but an on-going strike soon put an end to that, so he ended up spending the next few months as part of the crew aboard an offshore dragger.

Since his return home three months ago, he had been fishing off and on with Berton. When Donald had made his offer of a few days' work, he jumped at the chance to make a little extra money.

Now, as he walked out along the wharf toward the boat, it occurred to Gerald that, despite travelling across the country to get away from it, whether he was on the west coast or the east, the sea just seemed to keep trying to drag him back in.

His parents had thought they were being subtle about it, but they had both in their own way made it very clear that they were worried about him going out on the water tonight. His father had mentioned more than once the several official warnings he had received about the approaching storm, and his mother had kept coming up with just one more reason to delay his return to town.

Oh, well, Gerald thought as he swung his legs out over the edge of the wharf and started down the ladder to the boat, *just another couple of weeks and Carolyn and I will be off on our way to a new life.*

He wasn't too sure where or what this new life would be, but he hoped his mother would feel better about him finally being off the water.

5: A sudden flash of light

As Donald finished securing the boat to the crib-work, he noticed the first few specks of snow.

Tiny, fine, sparkling white flakes were falling on the back of his hand as he looped the rope around the cleat, and also on the deck, and on the scales of the day's catch in the fish kid. Little white crystals lit on the surface of the harbour water and floated there for just an instant before they vanished. A light dusting of snow was collecting on the back of Gerald's red-checked flannel shirt as he stood, bent over, unscrewing the cap to the gas tank.

Maybe the old man was right, maybe that storm is arriving sooner than expected.

Looking around, Donald saw the flakes materialize like magic out of the black night sky, flaring into life as they passed from the darkness into the brilliant glare of the dual floodlights mounted on the wall of the hoisting shed above, then gently wafting straight down undisturbed through the cone of light.

So, he thought, *no wind to speak of yet, just a little snow; no real indication of bad weather arriving any time soon.*

They were just tying up at Raymond's wharf to sell out their catch from earlier in the day, and to fuel up in preparation for the night ahead. Overhead, a heavy-duty electric motor whined to life and a steel cable unwound, lowering a 'bucket'—in reality, more like a steel half-barrel—onto the deck.

Donald grabbed his two-pronged pitchfork and began to toss fish into the bucket, being careful to pick out only the haddock from the three different species in the box. Pollock, cod, and haddock all went for different prices, so they had to be loaded and weighed separately.

In short order, Gerald had finished topping off the gas tank, unseen hands had pulled the long gas hose back up into the hoisting shed, and the last bucket of fish was hoisted off the deck.

The empty bucket soon reappeared with a receipt for the fish and a bill for the gas attached. It paused suspended in mid-air for a second while Donald re-trieved the papers, then rapidly disappeared upward into the glare of the lights.

As the *Ruth Lillian II* pulled away from the wharf, slipping out from under the floodlights, the water where the boat had been lit up, illuminating the long fronds of seaweed and kelp lazily waving back and forth on the harbour bottom ten feet below the surface, and giving the swirls left by the propeller an eerie green glow.

Suddenly the building was plunged into darkness. The hoist operator was done for the day; they had been his last customers.

Heading back down the harbour towards the lights of the breakwater a few hundred yards away, Donald was cruising between the ends of the wooden wharves that lined the waterfront atop their underpinning of tall posts, and the long line of fishing boats moored just offshore. He was just about ready to head out now. The only thing left to do was to pick up the trawl.

The ferry slip, a concrete ramp attached to the north side of the breakwater, was a handy spot for loading and unloading gear from a fishing boat. The ferry stopped running at dark and was usually tied up for the night farther out along the wharf, at a spot beyond the low-water mark, leaving plenty of room for a boat to pull up beside the empty slip at a point where it was more or less level with the sloping ramp, so it was easy to transfer items straight across and into the boat.

Figure 5: The Westport ferry

Donald noticed that tonight the approach to the slip was completely clear. In preparation for the expected storm, the ferry had been moved around to the sheltered south side of the wharf.

As they approached the wharf, under the flood-lights that lit up the ferry ramp and the surrounding water, he could see their trawl tubs lined up on the edge of the slip, ready for pick-up.

Walt Titus, a fisherman who lived just up the lane from the wharf, was returning from checking the lines on his boat. Seeing them approach, he stopped to lend a hand loading the tubs aboard. "You boys planning on heading out tonight?"

"Yeah, we had a pretty good haul last night, so we thought we'd give 'er another try tonight."

"You think that's a good idea? There's a big nor-easter heading this way, you know."

"It's still a ways off. Not supposed to hit 'til after daylight. We should be back in well before the weather gets too dirty."

"Well, I think you're pressing your luck. I hope you know what you're doing."

With the last tub loaded, Walt headed back up the ferry slip as Donald kicked the boat into gear and pulled away. Reaching the top of the slip, Walt turned to watch them go.

The *Ruth Lillian II* was pushing out two lines of wake from her bow and her propeller was leaving a glistening trail along the surface of the harbour. The air was completely still.

"Not as much as a breath of wind." he muttered to himself.

Walt had witnessed similar scenes countless times before, but on this night the sight of the boat slipping out from under the floodlights and gradually fading from sight behind a curtain of softly-falling snow left him with a sense of unease.

As they rounded the end of the wharf, Donald aimed the bow of the *Ruth Lillian II* toward Southern Point and the passage that would take them out into St. Mary's Bay.

Figure 6: Gerald Welch

Gerald busied himself with shifting the trawl tubs into their proper places and checking that the equipment that they would need later tonight was all in order. After a few minutes, he felt a familiar, smooth rise and fall under his feet, and looked up to see that they were approaching Little Passage. This passageway between Brier Island and nearby Peters Island produced a near-constant undulating swell, the result of the strong flow of tide which funnelled through this narrow opening.

Through the darkness and the snow, below the flashing beacon of the Peters Island light, Gerald could just make out the white, octagonal shape of the tower and the boxy outline of the lightkeeper's house. Now unoccupied, this had been his family's home for eleven years. His brother Berton had been born in that house, making him the only person to ever have "Peters Island" listed as his official place of birth.

Gerald himself had never lived there. By the time he was born, the family had moved over to the village of Westport and a house on Gull Rock Road.

After spending so many years on the tiny island, Percy and Ada had found the isolated location was just getting to be too much for their growing family to deal with. Travelling back and forth across the passage five days a week so the kids could attend school, then again on Sunday for church and Sunday School, and occasionally again to catch the Saturday night show at Gerald Strickland's little movie theatre, or maybe for a social gathering at the church vestry or the Oddfellows Hall, it all got to be just too impractical and risky.

Especially in winter, or during the fall storm season, there were many days when Percy would be unable to make the crossing safely, which meant the kids would have to miss school; or sometimes the wind would come up during the day and he'd not be able to get back over to pick them up in the afternoon. When this happened, the children would be on their own to seek out a relative or friend who could put them up for the night.

Not that they minded all this; the isolation and freedom to roam their own little island, the missed school days, getting storm-stayed on one island or the other, unexpected sleepovers—it was all a big adventure to the kids. But for Ada and Percy, even though there was no denying the uniqueness and charm of their little island empire, the remoteness created some practical problems and too many opportunities for their growing kids to get into mischief.

With four children to consider, and more on the way, Ada and Percy decided the sensible thing to do was move across the passage to Brier Island.

Since Percy still continued in his position as the Peters Island lightkeeper after the move, he had to spend extended periods of time on the island by himself. In case of an emergency, there was a phone on the island; but it was not reliable. The line was often blown down and damaged by stormy weather, and occasionally, in the fall deer hunting season, by getting tangled in the antlers of deer that would swim to the island to escape hunters.

Percy had a system in place in case he was in need of help and the phone was out. He would hang a red blanket on the clothes line as a distress signal. Gerald remembered how it was the job of the kids in the family to keep an eye out for that red blanket.

Although Gerald didn't grow up there, the family would move back to Peters Island for a time each summer, so he did get to enjoy some of the same experiences the older kids talked about, like playing in the rooms of the big old house with the dangerous upper story balconies, hiding under a bed in a safe inner part of the house while windows were being blown in and doors ripped off during one of the frequent August gales, knowing where to avoid the strong tides while swimming in the ice-cold water off the little beach, fishing off the rocks, slipping and sliding over the seaweed-covered shore to pick dulse and then drying it on the porch roof, and the some-times-scary ordeal of using the outhouse, perched near the edge of a windy cliff.

These adventures all came to an end when, after seventeen years, Percy was re-assigned to Northern Light on Brier Island. It wasn't as much fun for the kids, but it made getting to work a lot easier for Percy.

Gerald was jolted from his memories by a sudden flash of light. Donald had his spotlight trained on an-other boat that was heading into the passage just as they were coming out into St. Mary's Bay.

Recognizing the *Nat-Wen-Aann*, Gerald glanced at his watch: 10:05. Franklin was running a bit late to-night; the fishing must have been good to keep him out this long after dark.

Aboard his boat, Franklin Gower flashed his own spotlight in reply to the *Ruth Lillian II* and asked himself where those young fellers could be going at this time of night. He hoped it wasn't far.

Most of the other boats had long ago headed in. This weather was about due for a change, and not for the better: Franklin's bones and twenty-some years of experience on the water were rarely wrong about that.

6: Slim to none

Thursday, December 19

The Southwest Ledge lies about ten miles to the south and a bit west of Brier Island. Donald and Gerald arrived just after midnight. They were fishing at night because the wind usually drops out and the haddock bite better at night—at least that's what the old-timers believed. In this case, Donald decided he was willing to take advantage of their knowledge.

Judging by the compass heading he'd followed, the length of time they had been steaming, and the image of the ocean bottom that appeared on his depth sounder, Donald figured that they were more or less in the same spot where they had found good fishing the night before. Despite the predictions, the wind had picked up a bit by now and the stiff breeze was producing a pretty fair chop on the water, but that raised no concerns. A little rough water wasn't out of the ordinary for this far out.

He cut the engine back to an idle and shouted over his shoulder, "Okay! Get it over the side!"

Figure 7: Donald McDormand

Gerald dropped an anchor and the attached high-flyer into the water. As the boat idled along, he kept a close eye on the trawl line while the weight of the anchor and the movement of the boat pulled it steadily out of the tub. It looked like Everett had done a good job: the main line was neatly coiled in the tub and the gangens, those short lines, each with a baited hook on the end, that were attached to the main line at regular intervals, were pulling out without tangling.

The exact length and spacing of the gangens varied according to which species of fish you were trying to catch. They were looking for haddock tonight, so the gangens were twenty-four inches long and tied thirty inches apart. When they were fishing for halibut, a much larger fish, the gangens were made of a heavier cord, and were a fathom, or about two meters, in length and tied a fathom apart. Preparing correctly for the species you were trying to catch was important. If the trawl wasn't put together correctly, it could negatively affect your catch; and if the tub wasn't loaded properly, the trawl would sometimes come out in a big snarl.

Bracing himself up against the stern rail next to the trawl tub, Gerald used a stick to lift the line as it came out of the tub and, with a continuous flipping motion, tossed it over the back of the boat into the water. This helped keep the trawl from snarling up, and kept the gangens with their dangling, baited hooks from snagging on each other or the edge of the tub, or catching on the rail as they went over the side. It also gave him a little safe distance from those hooks.

Hooks were the cause of most of the injuries that occurred aboard a fishing boat. The large, heavy-duty, curved and twisted Mustad hooks were extremely sharp and could easily tear through the meat of an arm or leg, or pierce through a hand. Most captains kept a pair of wire cutters handy for removing a barbed tip that had hooked into some piece of flesh.

Since in most cases it couldn't be pulled back out if the tip didn't go all the way through whichever part of the body it had caught, the hook would sometimes have to be deliberately pushed the rest of the way through until the barb emerged and could be cut off.

Setting trawl is a bit easier than hauling trawl. It takes less time and less effort to set it than it does to haul it back again; but still, even with Donald leaving the wheel to help out, they were well into the night before they got it all set.

By the time the last tub had been emptied, the earlier breeze had picked up into a moderate wind, punctuated at increasingly-frequent intervals by stronger gusts. The snow was coming in at a slant now, and had turned into big, wet, annoying flakes that seemed to plaster themselves to everything in sight.

The earlier light chop had now developed into moderate-sized waves that were slapping up against the hull, causing a constant fore-and-aft rocking motion as well as an uneven, jerky, side-to-side roll that Donald and Gerald unconsciously compensated for as they moved around the boat.

Normally, with all their gear now in the water, this would be the time to give themselves a bit of a break and allow the trawl a little more time to fish. On any other night, they'd head down to the cuddy and grab a bite to eat, maybe fire up the little cabin stove and warm up a bit with a mug of tea or instant coffee, maybe even get off their feet in the bunk for a few minutes.

But not tonight. Tonight they could both see the obvious first indicators of the bad weather that was coming their way. They knew the storm was quickly starting to build, time was running short, and they had to start hauling their gear back right away.

Arriving back at the spot where they had set out that first trawl, they quickly picked up the high-flyer and began pulling in the line.

Donald was pleased: most of the hooks were coming back with a good-sized fish attached. It looked like this was going to be even better than last night's haul.

Over the next few hours, the weather continued to deteriorate. By the time they had managed to locate, lose, and then relocate that last marker, the wind was arriving in squalls, clipping the whitecaps off the waves that were tossing the *Ruth Lillian II* around like a matchstick.

The snow was streaming in horizontally now, blustering across the open deck with a stinging force that made any exposed bare skin feel like it was being sand-blasted. The trawl tubs had to be lashed in place to keep them from slamming back and forth, and loose gear thumped and clanged as the boat rolled wildly back and forth.

From his position at the wheel, Donald reached over and hooked the sliding cuddy door to stop it from banging open and shut with each roll of the boat.

It was going to be one hell of a job to get this gear back. Donald gave brief consideration to the idea of leaving it in the water in the slim hope that it would still be there whenever he was able to get back to it. In his estimation, the odds that there would be anything left for him to find after the storm died out in a couple of days ranged all the way from slim to none. He couldn't really afford to lose that much gear, not to mention all the fish it had most likely caught.

The storm was still building. It hadn't really hit full-force yet, and he figured they might still have time to haul their gear back if they were quick about it.

As it turned out, getting this line back took much longer than they had hoped. Normally the two of them would share the work, but the worsening weather made it unwise to leave the wheel for more than a few seconds at a time, so Donald was only able to help out briefly, and only when absolutely necessary.

They switched jobs periodically, giving Gerald a bit of a break during his turn at the wheel; but in the end, he did the majority of the grunt work by himself. He struggled, even with the assistance of the hauler, to bring in the line with its burden of fish, fighting the whole way against the jerking and yanking of the boat and the tugging of the waves.

Slatting the fish off the hooks, then attempting to coil the line back into the tub without making a complete mess of it, it seemed to take way longer than it should.

Finally, the last fish was hauled in over the side, the second buoy and anchor retrieved, and the last piece of gear stowed.

Exhausted, Gerald slumped down on the engine box and gave Donald the nod he'd been waiting for. "We're done. Let's head for home."

7: The darkest part of the night

The glowing amber dial of the marine radio that sat on the table beside Ace's living room chair cast a dim light across the overflowing ashtray where he ground out the stub of his cigarette. He automatically moved to pick up the next one, then thought better of it and withdrew his hand from what remained of the neat row that he had laid out in front of the radio.

It was not even two hours ago that he had rolled himself a dozen smokes. Now he only had three left.

Ace hadn't had much luck getting any rest so far tonight. Not long after he'd turned in, he had been awakened from a fitful sleep by the sound of the wind scratching the over-grown canes of the dormant raspberry plant against the wooden shingles at the back of the house. He'd been sitting here alone in the dark ever since, listening as the wind in the eaves gradually increased to a howl and the groans of the creaking timbers of the old house became even more pronounced with every gust.

His living room window afforded him a pretty good view of the harbour, including the spot at the wharf where Donald would be tying up when he got back. Even through the now-swirling snow, and the frost that was slowly creeping in from the edges of the glass, he should be able to see the lights of any boat approaching the dock.

But so far, he hadn't seen anything, not a glimmer. And he hadn't heard anything on the radio either. Earlier on in the evening, well before he'd gone to bed around midnight, the airwaves had been busy, mostly boats reporting that they were leaving the fishing grounds, heading back to the islands, or farther up the Neck to home port at East Ferry or Little River.

But now there was only silence.

He was starting to get worried. Among all the earlier chit-chat there hadn't been so much as a word from the *Ruth Lillian II*, not a peep out of them since they'd left the harbour. *Dammit! Why did I let them go? Why didn't I push harder for them to stay in on a night like this?*

Of course, Ace thought, *pushing harder doesn't usually work well with Donald*. He had always had his own way of doing things. Ace had learned early on it was a lot easier to just go with the flow.

As a kid, Donald had not been one to let circumstances get in his way. They hadn't had a lot of money to spend on toys and such back then, but when little Donnie and his friend Clayton showed up at Harris's Bluff on the back shore of the island, or up on the High Knoll on the road to Northern Light, to play Cowboys and Indians with the other kids, he was the one decked out with a lasso, a rifle, and six-shooters, all of his own creation.

Later on, he developed this knack for building his own toys into a talent for model-making. He and his friend Benny Verburgh shared an interest in making scaled-down versions of fishing boats, and made a practice of raiding Ace's buoy pile for material to use in building their model ships. Commandeering Ace's shop and tools, they split his wooden lobster buoys into two and carved each half into a surprisingly accurate replica of the boats they saw in the harbour.

As their skills increased, the two of them began cutting and planing down his new trap laths to make them into correct-sized planks for their models of sailing ships.

He remembered how they had worked for several weeks on a model of the schooner *Bluenose*, then decided to take it down to Pond Cove for its maiden voyage. After several test runs across the pond, the two boys felt confident enough in their sail and rudder settings to set her out on a longer trip across the open cove. One of them set the ship off from the point of land on one side of the cove, and the other retrieved it at the point on the other side.

They were extremely happy with how well the little vessel sailed and how well they were able to control her; that is until, on the second or third pass, the wind shifted a bit, just enough to cause their pride and joy to miss the far point by a few scant feet, just out of arm's reach. All they could do was stand and watch as their *Bluenose* headed out across the open ocean, sailing off alone in the direction of Bar Harbor.

As if depleting Ace's buoy and trap supplies was not enough, the boys then turned their attention to his punt. Ace recalled how the two of them had pounded his poor little boat full of nails, erecting a mast, rigging a bowsprit and a rudder, and fastening a keel to the bottom. For a flat-bottomed boat never meant for such a purpose, they got it to sail surprisingly well, and the two friends had a few days of fun roaming around the harbour until he finally needed to take his punt back.

Despite the high-jacking and misuse of his equipment, Ace hadn't really minded Donald and Benny's shenanigans. They were just two kids having some fun. In fact, he had been pleased to see Donald developing his talent and interest in model-making. Lord knows he wasn't much interested in anything else. He'd left school as soon as it was legally allowed, and joined his father fishing. Now, here he was with his own boat, and a determination to make himself known as one of the highliners in the village.

Ace had to admit to himself that he was proud to see his son's development as a fisherman. Just five or six years previous, the first summer of Donald seriously fishing with his father, the two of them had been working with the seining fleet. Donald had come down with a long-term stomach problem of some sort that mostly kept him confined to his bunk when he wasn't actually working.

For most teens his age, even for many adults, this would have been a perfectly valid excuse not to work, but Donald had shown up every time he was needed; never shirked his duty, never slagged off. Ace remembered how, on one August trip off Gannett Rock, despite being in obvious discomfort, his son had helped bring in thirty-four thousand pounds of pollock in one haul. It had been a good payday that week.

Although he would never say such a thing directly to his son, Ace admired Donald's ambition and drive, the way he was determined to not let anything stand in his way. But now he was starting to wonder if maybe Donald's enthusiasm and determination had blinded him to the danger of this situation and caused him to take on a risk he shouldn't have.

The weather had turned bad out there, and was getting worse by the minute. It was the darkest part of the night, the 'Always darkest before the dawn' time. Out on the road in front of his house, the blurry edges of the circle of illumination cast by the overhead streetlight shuddered back and forth on the growing snowdrifts as the wind continuously vibrated the arm at the top of the pole. Ace watched as a drift slowly crept across the road under the dim yellow light, stretching closer to the other side with each passing hour.

With a groan, Ace got up from his chair and stood at the window. He could feel a faint, cold draft blowing in around the frame.

Eileen had woken when he'd got up, but it seemed she'd fallen back asleep again. He considered calling his sister and her husband at Western Light to see if they had heard any news, but quickly decided against it. Even though he had no doubt they were up and worrying, too, they most likely had no information either, and the phone ringing at this time in the morning would probably not be a welcomed sound.

Ace grabbed the three remaining cigarettes off the table and tucked them into his shirt pocket, pulled on his coat and rubber boots, and headed out to his car. If the road was at all passable, he'd head down to Southern Point and see what he could see.

If they were able to make it home, they'd most likely be coming in through Little Passage.

8: Static with a different tone

Donald and Gerald were not on their way home.

They had attempted to start out in that direction, but quickly realized that the heading they were on had them quartering into the teeth of the now-raging storm. Continuous battering by heavy seas not only caused the *Ruth Lillian II* to shudder and falter in her tracks with every strike, but it felt like she was actually losing ground. The constant spray breaking over and across her bow was freezing on the windshield and cutting the already poor visibility to near zero, and the coat of heavy ice forming on the windward side of the boat was rapidly causing a worrying list to port.

They were also taking on a concerning amount of water over the side. They had the pump running non-stop, shooting a continuous stream out of the side of the boat, but it was not able to keep up with the water level in the bilge, which was slowly but steadily rising.

These factors, combined with the feeling that they were making very little real progress, if any at all, quickly made it clear to the cousins that the only smart thing for them to do in the circumstances was to make a run for the shelter of Yarmouth Harbour.

"Get on the radio," Donald ordered. "If you can raise anybody at all on that damn thing, let them know who we are and where we're heading."

The ship-to-shore radio situation aboard the *Ruth Lillian II* was less than ideal, to say the least. The radio that came with the boat had never really been reliable, and in the last few weeks it had gotten steadily worse. Most of the time, all they could receive were garbled transmissions interrupted by random noise and static; and when they tried to transmit, the microphone would work fine one minute, cut in and out the next, or not work at all.

Donald had hooked up a spare radio that Ace had lying around his shop, which he wasn't using because it had some issues of its own. By operating the two of them together, switching back and forth between the two radios, they were able to transmit and receive some of the time, but recently they had pretty much given up on trying to make it work.

Gerald keyed the button on the side of the mike and attempted to send out a message. He hoped that the radio would transmit properly, and if by some miracle it did, that there was someone close enough to hear it.

The area known as The Lurcher lies about thirteen miles offshore from Yarmouth, Nova Scotia, a little over twenty miles from Brier island, and ten miles or so from the *Ruth Lillian II*'s position southwest of Brier Island. It consists of two shoals, the Southwest and the Northeast, with water depths varying from a little over one fathom (about two meters) to about ten fathoms.

The two shoals, and the underwater banks around them, extend over several square miles. The makeup of the shoals, with broad shallow areas and sudden, deep drop-offs, makes them the ideal home and rich breeding ground for a variety of sea life.

The banks have long been a lucrative hunting ground for the famous Digby scallop fleet and for the Grand Manan herring seiners, and the deeper holes and drop-offs in the area invite those in search of several species of fish. The area can be productive as well for those lobstermen willing to venture a little further out and take a risk with their equipment during the stormy wintertime lobster season that has been allocated to this end of the province.

The Lurcher Shoals, like many places along the Atlantic coast, can lay claim to their own long history of shipwrecks. The tides flowing over and around the hidden ledges create strong and unpredictable currents that have caught many an unsuspecting sailor unawares. Since the shallowest part of the shoal remains about one fathom below the surface even at the lowest tide, there is little visual warning of the danger that lies in wait.

After decades of ships falling victim to these hidden dangers, it was proposed to the government that the Lurcher Shoals be marked with some sort of warning signal.

This proved to be no easy task. Being so far from land, and with no above-water base to build on, constructing a lighthouse on the site was not feasible. There were early attempts to set a beacon or buoy as an aid to navigation, but Atlantic storms, strong riptides, and the constant battering of the sea usually made short work of these endeavours.

One such example was an automatic whistling buoy, reported in place on December 31, 1883, anchored in thirteen fathoms of water east of the Lurcher Rock. Unfortunately, five months later it was found to be missing in action when the barque *L. H. Deveber* out of Saint John, NB, bound for Bristol with a load of lumber, struck on the Lurcher Shoal. The unlucky Capt. J. Willis Jones, of Weymouth, would eventually come to learn that the buoy that could have saved his ship had been discovered a month earlier, floating twenty-five miles off Cape Cod, Massachusetts.

In 1903, the Board of Trade at Saint John, NB requested that a lightship be stationed on the Lurcher Shoals "To assist in the safe guiding of passing vessels". In 1906, *Lurcher,* a steel steamer with three electric lanterns at the top of each mast and a diaphone foghorn powered by compressed air, was anchored off Lurcher Shoal.

Several generations of The Lurcher Lightship, unflatteringly described by one captain as "A mongrel —half ship, half lighthouse", would continue to stand guard for the next sixty-five years, until the last lightship, the *Lurcher 4,* was retired in 1969.

A vessel travelling from the vicinity of the Southwest Ledge, on a course to Yarmouth Harbour, is very likely to pass close to, or even over, the Lurcher Shoal and well within range of the Lurcher Lightship.

Aboard the *Lurcher 2*, Phillipe Dion had just noticed that the dial on the anemometer was indicating a wind speed of ninety miles per hour when he felt his stomach start to flip-flop. Phillipe thought, *Tabarnak! Here comes a big one!*

He grabbed the arms of his chair and hung on.

The ship rose as it was lifted by another huge swell, keeling over on its beam-ends to the point that

Phillipe felt he was about to fall backwards out of his seat. He tightened his grip, held his breath, and tensed in anticipation of what he knew was coming next.

Suddenly he was viciously jerked back upright as the *Lurcher 2* fetched up short on her massive anchor chains. Luckily, his chair was bolted to the radio room floor, as was the table that held his equipment.

Phillipe hated being tossed around like this. The Lurcher Lightship was well-known to be a miserable posting during stormy weather, and this storm was worse than most.

He had been monitoring radio traffic for most of the night; by now all of the boats should be in safe harbour somewhere, so there wasn't a whole lot to monitor, mostly just weather reports and static. And there was certainly no shortage of static. This storm seemed to be playing games with his radio equipment, and he hadn't picked up anything useful for a while now.

Night shift in the radio shack could be boring sometimes, with long hours of nothing much going on. Still, it was an important position. If an emergency arose, even though being fixed to one position meant there was not much real action the *Lurcher 2* could take to assist, the ship's powerful transmitter could be relied upon to relay needed information to the Coast Guard or to Search and Rescue.

Suddenly, Phillipe forgot all about his dodgy stomach. He snapped to attention as the continuous stream of static coming from the speaker was being interrupted by, well, more static. But this static had a different tone to it, and it sounded like there could be bits of words mixed in with it.

He pulled his headphones up from where they sat around his neck, clamped them over his ears, and listened intently as he tweaked the dial, trying to zero in on the frequency and bring in the message a little clearer, trying to make out the words.

Then, suddenly it was gone, the usual static resumed once again, and he was unsure of what he had heard. Was it a call for help, just someone chatting on the radio, or a freak bit of weather interference playing a trick on him?

Phillipe quickly keyed his mike and sent out a broadcast message, "This is the *Lurcher 2* to unknown vessel, *Lurcher 2* to unknown vessel, please repeat your message, please repeat your message."

He leaned forward in his chair and listened intently for a reply, pressing the headphone cups tight to his ears. All he got back was more static, mixed in with random noise.

For a few seconds he thought he again heard that odd bit of static, but this time there was nothing that could be interpreted as words, just the sound of electrical currents flying through the air.

Aboard the *Ruth Lillian II*, Gerald stared at the mike he was holding in his hand. "The damned thing just quit on me!"

"Are you sure? Click the button a couple more times. It doesn't always work on the first try. There's a loose connection or something."

"No, I tried that," Gerald replied, but he tested the key a few more times anyway. "It's completely dead, nothing but static. It was on its last legs anyway. All this banging around must have finished it off."

"Well, we should be in Yarmouth in a couple of hours. We'll find a phone and call home then."

"Why don't you let me take the wheel for a while? That harbour will be a bitch to get into in this weather; wouldn't hurt to take a break before you have to deal with it."

Donald didn't need to be asked twice. He took a quick glance at the compass, indicated that Gerald was to keep to the same heading, then turned the wheel over and ducked into the cabin.

Now that they had changed direction, the *Ruth Lillian II* was riding quite a bit easier. With the wind and the sea mostly coming from behind them, she was moving along at a pretty good clip.

Each huge swell that reared up behind the *Ruth Lillian II* lifted her stern as it approached and pushed her forward. Nose down, she sped along, surfing on the front of the wave. As the wave overtook and passed under her, she gradually levelled out and rose to its crest, where she hung among the foaming white water for what seemed like an eternity, the engine suddenly racing wildly as the propeller momentarily spun free out of the water, then biting again as she tipped backwards and slid down the back side of the wave as it sped on past beneath them.

It was a bit of a roller-coaster ride, not exactly comfortable, and a bit frightening at times when those waves looked like they were going to come right in over the stern, but at least now they weren't being slammed and tossed around like they were before.

In the cabin, Donald thought that if he braced himself a bit, he might even be able to get a bit of rest without being unceremoniously tossed out of his bunk.

At the wheel, Gerald was a little concerned about their chances of getting into Yarmouth in weather like this. He himself had only entered the harbour once before, a couple of years ago on a trip with Berton. He wished now that he had paid better attention to what his brother had said and done. He knew from listening to the stories of the old guys at home that Yarmouth Harbour was one of the safest and most protected harbours in this end of the province, but it could be a very tricky place to get into in a storm.

There were coves on both sides of the channel that were easy to mistake for the entrance, even in good weather. He seemed to recall that the one behind the Cape Forchu light was even called False Harbour Cove.

He did remember Berton telling him that you had to find and follow the channel that led into the harbour from quite a ways out. It was well-marked with buoys, but they might be hard to see in this weather. If you strayed out of the deeper water, you risked being overtaken by a wave and swamped from behind.

Gerald continued to try the radio microphone every few minutes. After several futile attempts, he came to the conclusion that the loose wire or faulty connection that had been causing it to cut in and out must have finally let go completely.

When Donald eventually reappeared to resume his place at the wheel, Gerald unplugged the cord and took the microphone down into the cabin with him.

Glad of the opportunity to get out of his oilskins for a bit, he stripped them off and laid them on the row of lockers that ran along one side of the hull and served double-duty as storage space and seating area. He lifted the lid of one of the lockers and rummaged around in a box of tools until he found the screwdriver he was looking for. He closed the lid, sat down on it, then hitched himself over behind the little table and braced his back against the inside curve of the hull.

As he started disassembling the microphone, his eyes began to droop. The bunk that Donald had just crawled out of looked pretty inviting. It was going to be a while yet before they were approaching Yarmouth, shouldn't be a problem if he just lay down for a minute or two. The microphone could wait.

Gerald awoke with a start. He checked his watch. Damn! He had been asleep for nearly an hour. They should be in Yarmouth Harbour by now, but judging by the movement of the boat, they weren't out of the storm yet. In fact, if anything, it seemed as if the weather had gotten worse. They must be getting close, at least.

He cracked the door open enough to shout out to Donald, "Any sign yet?"

"No, nothing yet. Been looking for the Cape Forchu light, but visibility's the shits. If the compass is right, we gotta be close. It'll soon be daylight, I should be able to see the coastline any time now if we're anywhere close to it."

Gerald slid the door closed and sat down at the table again. He picked up the broken mike and looked at it absently.

This didn't feel right. He was sure they should have reached port by now.

The *Ruth Lillian II* was not equipped with radar; the only navigation aids they had were a couple of old charts and an even older compass.

Gerald put down the mike and reached for his oilskins. *Better get back out there; an extra pair of eyes might come in handy right now.*

9: A particular wave

According to age-old mariner lore, ocean waves tend to come in repeating patterns. Popular legend says that among every set of so many waves there is one wave that is bigger than the others. Some say it's every third wave, some say every seventh.

The truth is that it can be anywhere between those two numbers. Except for tsunami-type waves, which are created by earthquakes or some other sudden geological disturbance, most waves are created by the effects of the wind. Generally speaking, the stronger the wind, the bigger the wave.

On the open ocean, waves created by a specific wind source start out more or less identical in size and shape. With about the same height and spaced about the same distance apart, waves tend to travel in groups called 'trains', and these trains can travel for surprising distances.

As they traverse the ocean, trains encounter other trains of waves which were created from other wind sources. When a wave from one train comes in contact with a wave from another train, depending on the relative size and frequency of the two waves and how they interact, they can detract from each other, in effect, cancelling each other out, thus decreasing the power of both of them, sometimes to the point that all that is left of their meeting is a flat spot on the ocean surface.

Or the reverse can happen. They can complement each other, joining and adding together to create a new and better wave, bigger than either of the two originals.

Closer to shore, shallow-water waves tend to travel faster than the deeper-water ocean waves. When deep-water waves reach an area of shallow water, they can speed up, and as they interact with local waves, combine to form a yet larger, faster wave.

Sometimes these additions build on each other and multiply several times to create a wave that can rise to a height that cannot be sustained. The white crest often seen at the top of large breakers indicates that the wave is disintegrating as it attains its maximum height. It has reached the point beyond which it is unable to maintain its own integrity.

Birthed off the New England coast of the United States by the first tentative winds of what was soon to become a vicious nor'easter—what some of the old-timers used to call a Nebraska Gale—one particular wave had been travelling for many hours and miles now. Up the Gulf of Maine, across the Bay of Fundy, and past the mouth of St. Mary's Bay it came, raging on. Pushed along by ever-increasing gales, ravenously feeding off of other waves it encountered along the way, adding to its strength, building and growing in fierceness with every mile, like a predator on the hunt, it rolled on.

Bursting out of the darkness into the storm-greyed pre-dawn light, the wave drove ever forward, towering over even the largest of its brethren, flinging wind-driven trails of foaming white spindrift from its crest like spittle from the maw of a rabid dog, constantly building and collapsing ever forward, consuming everything in its path. It sped mindlessly onward, on course to make direct landfall among the Tusket Islands.

Not far ahead, the *Ruth Lillian II* motored on.

10: We got to make the call

Ace gunned the engine in his old car and took another run at the snowdrift that blocked the short road that led out to Southern Point. The roadmaster for the island, Brad Delaney, had been out clearing snow with his ancient Caterpillar tractor since before daylight, bucking through the drifts in the early darkness, but the snow was blustering back in just as fast as he could get it plowed out.

Luckily, this snowdrift was one of the smaller ones, and it only took Ace a couple of tries to push his way, engine roaring and tires spinning, through the dense, wind-packed snow.

He sidled his car up as close as he dared to the edge of the little turn-around area at the end of the road overlooking Peters Island, not much more than a stone's throw away on the other side of Little Passage. With the driver's side facing the drop-off to the rocks, and then to the waters of St. Mary's Bay beyond, he rolled down the car window, allowing in a gust of snow that scattered a layer of flakes across his dashboard.

Ignoring the freezing wind, as well as the occasional wind-carried drops of salt spray that managed to reach him from the waves breaking on the jagged basalt shoreline below, he leaned his head out of the window and peered straight ahead, looking off in the direction of the wind-lashed waters of St. Mary's Bay.

He'd already done this twice before in the last few hours with no result, but it had still been dark then. It had just come daylight now, at least as light as it was likely to get while this storm lasted. He hadn't seen anything in his earlier attempts, and he wasn't fooling himself: he didn't really expect to see anything this time. The daytime visibility now wasn't all that much better than it had been during the night. Ace knew that with this weather, it wasn't likely he'd be able to see anything, and even less likely that there would actually be anything out there for him to see.

This couldn't even be considered a long-shot, far from it. He knew he was just wasting his time on a fool's errand. Deep down, he didn't really expect to see anything; but this was all he had, he didn't know what else to do.

He shut off the engine and leaned a little further out the window. Turning so his ear was toward the direction in which he had been looking, Ace closed his eyes and concentrated, hoping, but again, not really expecting, to hear the far-off sound of a boat engine.

But the only sounds that came to him were the howling of the wind, the crashing of the waves, and the intermittent, drawn-out drone of the Peters Island foghorn. The normally ever-present screeching of seagulls was conspicuously absent.

Ace shook his head at this realization. *Even the damn seagulls know better than to come out in this weather.*

After a minute or two, he rolled up his window and started the car, then sat dejectedly while it rocked and creaked on its springs as the wind whipping over this exposed point buffeted it. He sat there for a long time, watching the snowflakes on his dash turn into little pools of water as the car's heater did its job.

He didn't want to move from this spot. Wherever they were, this was likely as close to them as he was going to be able to get, maybe as close as he was ever going to get.

Ace was putting off taking the next step. He knew what that next step should be, but he really didn't want to do it. Once he made that move, there was no going back, no more denying the reality of the situation. Besides, it wasn't entirely his call to make.

He put the car in gear and followed his tire tracks back out. They were already starting to fade in the fresh snow.

A short time later, Ace came to a stop at the top of the hill where you make the turn onto the dirt road leading to Western Light. He paused to survey the situation.

He'd already started down this road earlier, but had only made it to the far end of the graveyard. From there on, once past the protection of the trees, the road had been solidly drifted in for as far as his high-beams could show.

He'd got stuck there for a few minutes, trying to turn around in the deep snow, but now it looked like Brad had just recently been through here with his plow. There was a freshly-made narrow swath cut through the drifts, just wide enough for one vehicle.

Half-way down the road, he came face-to-face with Brad coming back. The big, V-shaped plow on the front of his tractor seemed to take up the whole width of the road.

Brad backed up a bit, then veered over and rammed the plow into the waist-deep snow at the side of the road, the steel tracks of his tractor churning up a combination of ice and frozen gravel from the road surface. Finally, after several attempts, he was able to move over far enough to allow Ace to edge past.

At Western Light, Ace quickly rapped twice on the kitchen door, then entered without waiting for a response.

He found Ada and Percy sitting at the kitchen table, each with a half mug of long-ago-gone-cold coffee in front of them. The oil lamp in the centre of the table was still burning, even though it had been daylight for a while now. Ada had obviously been crying, and Ace thought Percy looked alarmingly grey and drawn.

"Have you heard anything?" Ada asked hopefully.

"No. You?"

"No, not a word."

"It's sure not looking good." Ace forced himself to say the words. "I suppose they might'a got into shelter somewhere, but I think since we ain't heard from 'em, we got to make the call."

"I suppose you're right." Percy spoke quietly without looking up. "If they could have made it back, they'd be here by now. And if they went somewhere else, why haven't they called? It's been long enough now. I'll call Search and Rescue."

He got up with an effort and walked over to where the phone hung on the wall. They still didn't have electricity at Western Light, but, thank goodness, the phone line had been run out to them a few years ago.

Ada began to sob. "I can't believe this is happening again!"

"Now, Ada." Ace tried as best he could to comfort his sister. "We don't know anything, not really. They may be fine. They just can't let us know for some reason or other."

The two sat in silence as they listened to Percy's side of the phone conversation. Finally, he hung up and returned to the table.

"That was the Search and Rescue in Halifax. They're not gonna report them as missing yet, just as overdue. I gave them a description of the boat and their last location, as far as we know it. They said the weather's too bad right now for an air search. They wouldn't be able to see anything, anyway. But they'll send out a plane from Greenwood Air Force Base as soon as it clears. They said all they can do for right now is put out a general bulletin asking people to keep a look-out for them."

Ada was not comforted by this news. "But this weather might not let up for days yet! Isn't there something more we can do?"

"Wait," said Ace. "All we can do is wait."

11: Luck's got nothin' to do with it

Raymond Robicheau had two stores, a big store and a little store. The little store was just across the road from what the locals called the breakwater, the government wharf that was the centre of much of the village's daily business. It was the perfect location from which to monitor not only the constant comings and goings of the Westport boats, but also the visiting Digby scallop fleet or the Grand Manan herring seiners who often used the islands as a base when they were fishing over in this part of the Bay.

The ferry dock was a part of the wharf, too. The first thing a visitor to the island saw upon reaching the top of the slip after driving off the ferry was Raymond's little store, dead ahead, right there across the street. Any traffic leaving the wharf had to stop and turn either left or right onto the main street, right there in front of the store. This made it a very convenient spot for keeping tabs on which strange cars were arriving on the island and which familiar ones were leaving.

The self-assigned responsibility for all this unofficial information-gathering fell to a small, informal group of six or seven retired or semi-retired island residents. At any time of the day or night, from eight o'clock in the morning when the store opened its doors, until ten at night when it closed—less the two hours when it was closed from twelve noon to one for dinner and then again from five to six for supper—at least two or three of these gentlemen (it was all gentlemen; no ladies were included in this group) could be found deep in discussion, enshrouded in a wreath of smoke from their ever-present cigarettes, pipes, and the occasional cigar, occupying their usual place on the old church pew that took up a good section of the store's north wall.

On a usual weekday, the crowd would be sparse, made up mostly of idlers and the elderly, but on this Thursday afternoon the bench was full to overflowing. The full gang of retirees was in attendance, and was supplemented with a goodly number of men and boys of all ages sitting on up-ended pop bottle crates and nail kegs, or, if they couldn't find a makeshift seat, leaning against the shelves that lined the walls.

As was usual any time there were two or more people in attendance, a variety of opinions were flying thick and fast. Usually, the topics under discussion could range anywhere from the potentially explosive field of politics, to the proper way to bait a hook, to why Squid Garron had painted his boat such a gawd-awful colour.

Some of the regulars had spent so much time at this, that they could almost be considered professional arguers, ever ready to take on any subject and more than eager to debate any side of it. These verbal duels might be resolved in a matter of minutes; or they could go on for hours, even days sometimes.

One veteran debater was famous for his ability to start out arguing for one side of a topic, then changing sides once he saw which way the wind was blowing, and campaigning just as sincerely for the opposite side, then vehemently declaring when challenged that he had never changed sides at all, that whatever the winning argument had been, that was the opinion he had held and championed all along. On a few noteworthy occasions, he had been known to successfully argue three sides of a topic, ending up back where he had started.

Depending on the subject, these verbal battles could be tedious, serious, interesting, and, on the rare occasion, even educational; but no matter the subject, the common denominator was a certain amount of sly wit and a good dose of wry humour that occasionally rose to the level of hilarity, sometimes intended, more often not.

But today the atmosphere around the bench was subdued. No one was cracking jokes. The conversation was definitely less boisterous and more respectful than usual, and centred on the one item of news that was occupying the minds of all who were in attendance.

Word spreads fast in a village of just over four hundred people: the *Ruth Lillian II* had failed to return.

The door opened and Dewie Frost stomped in, knocking the snow off his boots and bringing a flurry of snowflakes and a gust of cold air with him.

The crowd turned as one with a look of faint surprise. Dewie was a rare visitor to these parts. He lived down the road a ways and usually hung out on the bench at one of the other stores.

He approached the group and asked of no one in particular, "Any word of the boys yet?"

Walt responded for the group, "Nope! None that I've heard of anyway. Been lots of back-and-forth on the radio this morning. Search and Rescue's got a bulletin out, asking people to keep an eye out for 'em, but no one's seen a sign yet, far as I know."

"That doesn't sound good."

"No, it sure don't. Course, I don't know who's going to see 'em. There's nobody much out on the water in this weather."

"That's true."

"Coast Guard's the only ones might be equipped to be searchin' offshore in a blow like this, but last I heard, they haven't left the wharf. Search and Rescue considers the boat as being overdue, not missing, so I guess they're not doing a active search yet. I dunno, maybe that's a good sign; maybe it means they think that the boys are still afloat, that they still got a chance to make it back home under their own power."

From his spot on the bench, Lon Swift had been listening to the conversation, getting more agitated by the second. "Don't talk so damned foolish, Walt. It ain't a good sign, it ain't a good sign at all!"

"Why do you say that, Lon?" Walt asked, a little offended.

"Just take a look outside! It's been blowing a livin' gale ever since those boys went missing! The Coast Guard ain't gone out cause even they couldn't live out there now, so a small boat like theirs sure ain't gonna survive. They ain't lookin' cause they know more than likely there's nothing left to find! If that boat was still afloat don't you think it woulda turned up somewheres by now?"

"Well, visibility's not the best right now. Once the storm dies down, with any luck, they'll find them laid by in some shelter somewhere."

"Luck? Luck's got nothin' to do with it! It's a bad situation I'm telling ya. It ain't going to turn out good, that's for sure. No, it ain't going to turn out good at all."

"You think they went down?"

"Down? Of course they went down!"

"Don't you think they coulda maybe made it back inshore and took shelter in some little cove or something?" Dewie interjected hopefully.

"No. Shelter? No! If they did that, we woulda heard from them. They got a radio aboard that boat, don't they? Don't you think they'd of made a call and let someone know by now? No, there's no doubt about it, that boat's gone and those boys gone with it."

"Jeez, Lon, you're a real ray of sunshine!" said Walt, straightening up from adding another stick of wood to the little cast-iron stove that sat in the middle of the room and provided heat for the store. "You don't think they're still offshore and you don't think they made it inshore. You're not leaving a whole lot of room for hope here!"

From his place on the bench, Lon took a couple of seconds to flick his cigarette ash onto the floor and then scuff it into the wood with the sole of his rubber boot. He tilted his head up and peered out at Walt from under the brim of his tweed cap. "Hope? No, I guess I sure don't see no cause for hope. Now, don't get me wrong. I'd like to see them boys get home safe as much as the next man. I just don't see much chance of it happenin', is all."

The mood in the room had turned even gloomier than before. Everyone else was uncharacteristically quiet as they listened to the conversation.

"What makes you so sure about that?" Dewie ventured. "They got a good boat under 'em! Those Cape Islanders are built for bad weather. I seen 'em come through storms lots worse than this."

"It ain't just the boat. I remember my first winter fishin' with my father, we was trawlin' out near the Lurcher Shoal."

The assembled group exchanged glances, some with discreet eye-rolls. Most of them had heard various versions of this same story numerous times before.

Under normal circumstances, the group would have stopped Lon right here, but these were not normal circumstances. Dewie was not one of the regular gang, the story might have some actual relevance this time, and Lon was not one to easily pass up an opportunity to tell one of his favourite stories to someone who didn't know it by heart.

"Well," he continued, "we just got our lines set out when the wind started pickin' up. I wanted to keep at it, but the ol' man says dirty weather's comin' in fast and we gotta haul our gear back b'fore it hits. We had six skeins in the water, and by the time we got the fourth one back aboard we was gettin' slatted around so bad it was all we could do to keep our feet under us! Wind so fierce it was drivin' the spray off the water like buckshot, stingin' your eyes so you could hardly see. I wanted to hang in there and haul those last couple'a lines, but the ol' man says he'll be damned if he'd be drowned for a few fathoms of cod line, so we just abandoned our gear right there, never saw it again. Probably lost a good haul of fish along with it, too."

"So what'd you do then?" Dewie asked with genuine interest. "Head for home?"

"Home? No, we didn't head for home. Like now, it was blowin' from the sou'west, and the ol' man said we'd just beat ourselves to death trying to steam into the wind. We didn't have no choice but to turn and run with the wind, so that's what we did. We pounded our way along in the pitch black for a couple hours, and just about the time I'm startin' to think I'm never goin' to see land again, I catch a flash from the Yarmouth light. I tell you, mister, I was never so damned glad to see a light in all my life. I figured now we had our bearin's, we were gonna be all right. Then I hear a roarin' and a crashin' and straight ahead of us all's I can see looming up in the dark is a long line of white, what looks like a solid wall of surf breaking along the shore."

"So you weren't near the harbour after all, Lon?" someone from the crowd prompted, knowing full well the answer.

Everyone present was thoroughly familiar with the approach to Yarmouth Harbour. Any boat from either island, if caught out in a storm in the lower part of the Bay and unable to make for home, would head for safe haven at Yarmouth; they'd all done it at some time or other.

Still, Lon carried on as if imparting an important piece of information that only he was privy to. "I figured we musta missed the entrance somehow. Myself, I would'a turned around right there, but the ol' man's at the wheel. I yelled and pointed towards the surf on the shore, but he never moved a muscle, never flinched, never gave no sign he even heard me, just hung onto that wheel and headed straight t'wards that line of surf. I thought fer sure he was gonna pile us up on the beach and we'd get beat to death on the rocks. Then, next thing I know, there we are inside the harbour."

"So I guess your ol' man knew what he was doin' after all." Dewie was caught up in the story.

"Yeah! That's the thing of it. Turns out it's a real shoal bottom off that harbour. Any bad weather from the sou'west drives these big rollers in from way off-shore."

"How'd you manage to avoid being overtaken by those waves?"

"Well, you see, the channel into that harbour is narrow, real narrow, but it's deep. Keep dead in the middle of it and you're okay, but run off to either side into that shallow water and you'll get swamped fer sure. The ol' man knew that."

Walt saw an opportunity to cut the story short by jumping in with a question. "Don't you think maybe them boys could have done the same thing, then?"

"No! Done it? No! That's what I'm saying, don't you see? It was only the ol' man's knowledge and experience that saved us that day. Just about every decision I would'a made on that trip was the wrong one. Any one of them bad decisions would'a got us drowned. I would'a piled us up on the beach trying to enter that harbour. I didn't then know what my father knew. I was too young, too green back then. Just like them two boys."

"You know," Walt said, "I believe I was the last person to see those boys alive."

Realizing what he had just said, Walt corrected himself. "What I mean is, I was probably the last to see them *leave*. I watched them go out. Beautiful, calm night, not a breath a wind, water smooth as glass."

"Sure sign of a storm comin', when the air's that still," Lon observed.

"What I don't understand," Walt replied, "is why they'd go so far offshore with the weather report callin' for a blow? Hell, why go out at all? Everybody knew that storm was on its way. I told them myself it was a bad idea. Even his own father told them not to go out!"

Lon exhaled noisily through his teeth. "You know as well as I do why they went! You got two young bucks, one of 'em with a new wife to look after, tryin' to make a little extra money with Christmas comin' up. Donald only had that boat a few months, got payments due, fuel to pay for, gear to pay for, bills to pay for...all the same reasons any fisherman goes out."

Several discussions broke out at this point, but quickly fell silent again as the door opened and Ace entered. He walked to the counter, seemingly without noticing the unusually large crowd that was suddenly preoccupied with cleaning the ashes out of the bowls of their pipes, or had developed a deep interest in some product sitting on one of the shelves, or giving their full and undivided attention to rolling a smoke—anything to make it seem like they weren't giving him undue notice.

Ace tossed two quarters on the counter. "Pack of Player's Plain."

The day clerk, Gladys Baily, who had already anticipated Ace's usual order, paused with a pack of Player's rolling tobacco in her hand. "You don't want makin's? You want ready-mades?"

"Yeah. My hands are shakin' so much lately I can't even roll a cigarette."

Now that Gladys had broken the ice, from across the room Walt spoke up. "How you bearin' up, Ace?"

Ace sauntered over to the group as if it was just any other day. "As well as can be expected, I guess. Just waitin' to hear something, you know? Eileen's havin' a rough time of it, though. Longer it goes on, the tougher it is to keep her hopes up."

No one spoke. Everyone was waiting for someone else to respond.

Finally, Ace himself broke the silence with a sigh. "I dunno what to think, boys. To tell you the truth, the situation's lookin' pretty black right now."

"It'll look better in the morning." Lon spoke with a reassuring tone of voice. "This wind's supposed to drop out overnight tonight. The boats'll be able to get out tomorrow, somebody's bound to find 'em. They're probably just holed up somewhere, waitin' out the storm."

Walt turned and looked at Lon with an expression of surprise.

"Maybe so," Ace responded, grasping for a little hope among an abundance of doubt. "But if they made harbour somewhere, why hasn't anyone seen them?"

"Why, they might not be in a harbour at all," Lon said. "They might'a missed Yarmouth altogether, went right past and ended up farther down around Wedgeport. Easy to do in a storm. There's lots of isolated little islands and coves down that way; some of them have wharves and shacks on 'em, they coulda got out'a the wind in behind one of those islands and might be tied up at one of the wharves right now. Or maybe they're just layin' to in the lee of the land somewhere, waitin' for this storm to die down some."

"If that's the case, why haven't they reported in?"

"Well," Lon said, "the boys here say that radio of theirs hasn't been all that reliable even at the best of times. In this dirty weather, it's probably gone on the blink again."

"Yeah, maybe you're right," Ace said. "They never did have much luck with that old piece of junk, and the one they got from me was in no better shape."

"Sure, that's all it is. They'll turn up once the weather clears."

"Well, I sure hope you're right. I can't stand much more of this."

Ace returned to the counter, picked up the pack of smokes and his sixteen cents change Gladys had placed there, and headed for the door. "I better get back home. Don't like to leave the ol' lady alone for too long."

As soon as the door closed, Walt turned to Lon, "Well, you sure changed your tune in a hurry!"

"Whattaya mean?"

"First you had us all just about convinced that those boys are on the bottom of the ocean, then all of a sudden you're giving Ace all kinds of reasons why they're going to be just fine."

Lon sat back on the bench and took a few seconds to mull Walt's statement over in his mind. Then, as if he had examined his own actions and found the right words to explain them, he replied, "Look, much as I hate to say it, there ain't a bit of doubt in my mind but that those boys have perished. But I don't see any good at all to come from Ace hearin' that! The man's at the end of his rope. The only thing in this world keepin' him afloat right now is one last little glimmer of hope. Until he hears otherwise, he can still believe there's a chance for them boys. He's hanging on to that little bit of hope for dear life. It's all he's got right now. I'm sure as hell not going to be the man that takes it away from him. He'll soon enough have no choice but to face up to the facts of the matter. For now, I don't see no harm in lettin' him hold onto that little bit of hope for a little while longer."

Walt slowly nodded. "Yeah, I guess you're right about that." He began to button up his coat. "Guess I'd better get for home, too. It's almost five. Gladys'll be closing up soon."

One by one, the assembled throng shuffled out, with Lon bringing up the rear behind the last few stragglers.

Gladys stood by the door with her boots and coat on, ready to lock up and head home for her supper. The store would open again in an hour, when Raymond would take over the clerking duties. "Bye, boys, see you tomorrow," she said. "Oh, and, Lon, that was a real nice thing you did there."

Lon just shrugged and stepped out into the storm.

12: A ray of hope

Friday, December 20

Ace stood staring vacantly out his living room window as night reluctantly gave way to day. He watched as the diluted winter light slowly revealed the smoothly contoured shapes of the snow drifts in his front yard. Sculpted by the same wind that created the waves out in the harbour, they looked similar in shape.

It was just on the slack side of high tide. Across the road, he could see the radio antennas of the boats whipping back and forth as they rocked and rolled in place where they were tied up on the lee side of the wharf. Not a boat in the harbour had moved from the wharf or left its mooring in the last day-and-a-half, and, by the looks of today's weather, they wouldn't be going anywhere any time soon.

Even though it was almost fully daylight now, the floodlights shining down from their poles still bathed the wharf in an artificial glow that was brighter than the surroundings. Ace was surprised that the lights were still working at all. Down on these islands, the first thing to go during a storm of any size was usually the power.

Ace yawned. He was feeling rough this morning. It'd been another long night. He hadn't even bothered to turn in this time; he knew he wouldn't be able to sleep.

The radio beside his chair was silent; he'd turned it off hours ago. There had been a fair amount of chatter about the boys, most of it from people speculating on where they might be, where they could have gone to find protection from the storm, what might have happened to them. Some people expressed hope and concern for the boys, even said prayers for their safety.

But there were also a few thoughtless comments, too:

> "It's too late to start looking now."
> "No way a boat could survive in that."
> "Can't believe they'd even go out in weather like that."
> "This is what happens when you don't know enough to come in out of a storm."

Ace had had enough; he couldn't listen to any more of that foolishness. Nobody had anything new to say, anyway, just the same old stuff he'd already heard a dozen times before—and he sure as hell didn't need any more of that negativity.

He took another sip of his lukewarm coffee. He had laced his last two cups with a little splash of rum. He'd doubled up on this one. It didn't seem to help.

Ace recalled that, somewhere, someone recently told him that the wind was supposed to drop out overnight. Well, that hadn't happened. The harbour was still dotted with whitecaps. It had been too rough all day yesterday for the ferry to cross and, by the looks of the spray flying over the wharf and the big waves regularly rolling up and back down the ferry slip, it would most likely be out of commission again today.

But, he thought, *it isn't looking all bad*. Although it was still blowing a pretty good gale outside, the wind wasn't nearly as strong as before.

He'd noticed that over the last couple of hours the old timbers of his house had been doing a lot less creaking and groaning. The snow had let up quite a bit, too. This morning's sky was now looking brighter, and visibility through the thinning snow was much better. Ace could now just make out two of the three houses that perched on the hill above Roney's Point over in Freeport, across the passage.

Maybe if things continue to improve, the Greenwood Air Force Base will be able to get a plane up before the day is over.

From out in the kitchen, Eileen called him to come have something to eat.

As Ace took his place at the table, across from where Donald usually sat, Eileen put his breakfast down in front of him, then picked up a plate with two pieces of toast on it from the counter and settled into her own seat at the end of the table, the chair closest to the stove.

As the only woman in the house, now that her daughter Sylvia had left home for a job on the mainland, and as a person who naturally tended to keep her emotions to herself anyway, Eileen McDormand found it was not easy to share her private thoughts and feelings with two men, even if they were her son and husband.

Some people found Ace and Eileen to be a bit of an odd couple, both in appearance and personality. Eileen was a little on the larger side physically, while Ace was of a more wiry build. Although he himself was not one who could easily express his emotions, Ace was the more outgoing and sociable one of the two. A frequenter of the store bench, he was not at all shy about presenting his opinions to anyone who would listen. In contrast, Eileen, who seemed to be comfortable with her relatively solitary life, was rarely seen outside of her house and, for the most part, only spoke to her nearest neighbours.

Despite the differences, or perhaps because of them, the couple had been able to make it through some tough times. Only four years earlier, their house had caught fire and burned down in the middle of the night, leaving them with not much more than the clothes on their backs. The four of them, Ace, Eileen, Donald, and Sylvia, had moved in with Ace's father, "Billy Mac", in his house down the road near the wharf.

Then, just eleven months after that, on a sunny September Sunday morning, Ace's boat had caught fire and burned at its moorings in the harbour. Donald had been aboard at the time and suffered burns to his face and hands. Luckily, his cousin David, Gerald's brother, had been passing by in the *Elaine D.* and managed to pull Donald to safety just before the boat was fully engulfed in flames.

Eileen hadn't had a lot to say on those occasions, and, true to form, she wasn't saying too much now.

In silence, Ace took a bite or two of his breakfast, realized he didn't have much of an appetite, and pushed his dish away. He glanced over at Eileen, who sat staring vacantly at Donald's empty chair, absent-mindedly tearing her toast into tiny bits.

Finally, she seemed to focus and glanced over at Ace. "Do you think we'll hear anything today?"

"I don't know. The wind might drop out later today, so maybe they'll finally get a search plane up. Looks like the worst of the storm's over; maybe they'll be able to get a boat out then, too."

Ace stood up. "I can't spend the rest of the day just sitting around. I gotta find out what's going on. There's gotta be something we can do to get things movin'."

Raymond Robicheau's second, bigger, store was down the road a ways from the little store. It was built out over the water, right at the foot of the New Lane, the road that led up the hill to where the road to Western Light branched off. He was sitting at the desk in his crowded little office at the back of the store when he heard footsteps approaching.

He swivelled around in his chair to see a haggard, rumpled, unshaven, red-eyed figure standing in the open doorway. Putting the phone receiver he was holding back on its cradle, he greeted his visitor. "Ace! I was just about to call you!"

"What about? Did you get some news? Did they find something?"

Raymond could see the mixture of hope and dread on Ace's face, "No, no, nothing's been found yet. I just got off the phone a few minutes ago with Search and

Rescue. They expect the wind to drop off enough this afternoon that they should finally be able to send out a search plane. So that's some good news, I guess."

"What about the boats? Have they got any boats out yet?"

"I don't know, but I can damn soon find out."

The old wooden office chair creaked and rolled on its casters as Raymond swivelled around to face the wall and the wooden telephone box that hung there. He cranked the little handle on the side of it. They were still using the old-style phone system down here on the islands—it would be one of the last places in the province to be converted to dial-up.

Pushing a little black button while turning the crank got the operator over in Freeport on the line. "Elsie, has anyone talked to the Department of Transport in Saint John yet?"

In a situation like this, telephone operator Elsie Young was a valuable resource and a clearing-house of information. She sat in her living-room in front of her switchboard, and all long-distance calls and most of the local calls that were made on either island had to go through her. She knew who had talked to whom, and usually had a pretty good idea of what the conversation was about.

"No?" Raymond said. "No one talked to them yet? Okay, can you connect me?"

As Ace leaned against the door frame, once again listening in silence to a one-sided phone conversation, his mind slipped back to the news report he had heard over his car radio a few minutes earlier. Radio station CHSJ from Saint John had reported two fishermen from Brier Island missing in the Bay of Fundy.

Ace hadn't had time yet to decide how he felt about hearing that. It was upsetting to have their names announced on the radio. It somehow made it too real: now they were officially missing.

On the other hand, maybe this would bring them more attention and they'd finally start getting some real help.

Raymond hung up and turned back to Ace. "I talked to a Mr. McKinnon. He said they had the Coast Guard Buoy Tenders *Thomas Carlton* available in port in Yarmouth, and the *William Foster* in Saint John. The wind's finally dropped out some, and it's cleared up enough for them to be able to see a good distance, so he's ordering them both out right away."

A few minutes later, Ace was plowing his car through the many small snowdrifts that had formed across the road since his last trip down to Western Light. Raymond had been about to call Ada and Percy and fill them in on the latest news, but Ace stopped him. He wanted to be the one to tell them in person.

For the first time in the last forty-eight hours he felt like he finally had the opportunity to do something useful. The feeling of helplessness that was weighing so heavily on him lifted somewhat, now that he had a bit of good news to share. He knew it wasn't much, but it was all he had to contribute for now.

Ada and Percy, both looking even more worn-out than the last time he saw them, were relieved and cautiously encouraged to hear Ace's report. Maybe now that concrete action was finally being taken, the boys would be found.

Ace also relayed to them as much as he could remember of Lon's positive view of the situation. The three of them agreed that Lon could be right; it was entirely possible that the boys could have survived the storm, so there was cause to be optimistic.

This latest news of the search was definitely a ray of hope. Maybe their ordeal would all be over soon.

Later that afternoon, at four-fifty pm, the Yarmouth detachment of the RCMP received a phone call from a Mrs. Bradford Simmons. She was calling to report that a boat had been found washed ashore on one of the Tusket Islands.

13: A shipwreck near Outer Baldonia

The Tusket Islands are scattered along twenty miles of the Nova Scotia coast just south of Yarmouth. In fact, from the mouth of Yarmouth Harbour, on a clear day, you can just make out the first few islands in the group. Local legend has it that there are three hundred and sixty-five islands in the Tusket Group, one for each day of the year; some sticklers for accuracy claim the number to be more in the vicinity of two hundred and fifty.

The islands vary widely in size and shape, and they have a long and storied history. They first became known to Europeans in 1605, when Samuel De Champlain discovered them.

As is common with many coastal communities in Nova Scotia, there is the usual rumour of pirate treasure, although the exact location has so far not been identified. On one of the islands, aptly named Murder Island, numerous human remains have been found, the result, according to some, of a vicious battle, either between the Aboriginal residents of the area and white settlers, or between two warring tribes, the Iroquois and the Mi'kmaq.

Another theory to explain this gruesome discovery is that the bones are the remains of African slaves who were executed to keep secret the details of the underground treasure chamber they had constructed for their masters on nearby Oak Island.

Another interesting island, with a more recent story to tell, is Outer Bald Island. In 1948, Russell M. Arundel, an American sport fisherman who had arrived in the area to do some tuna fishing, took a liking to the island and bought it for $750 U.S. He had a stone cottage built on the island and, despite only ever spending one night there—he blamed that on the mosquitoes and relentless cold wind—he declared the four-acre island to be an independent nation and granted himself the title of Prince of Outer Baldonia.

The population of Arundel's micronation was men-only, comprised entirely of fishermen. Anyone who caught a tuna was granted citizenship; those who could pass a fishing test were granted royal titles.

As chairman of the Pepsi-Cola Bottling Company of Long Island, New York, Arundel had friends in high places who helped him promote his imaginary principality, and before long his self-declared nation was getting international attention and he was receiving invitations from well-meaning but oblivious foreign embassies. Tongue-in-cheek stories about this "tiny emerging nation" began to appear in various publications.

A magazine editor in the Soviet Union got hold of one of these stories and, under the mistaken belief that it was a serious piece of journalism, wrote a highly critical opinion of the Baldonian Constitution, which declared that its citizens were guaranteed "The right of freedom from question, nagging, shaving, interruption, women, taxes, politics, war, monologues, cant, and inhibitions. The right to applause, vanity, flattery, praise, and self-inflation. The right to swear, lie, drink, gamble, and silence. The right to be noisy, boisterous, quiet, pensive, expansive, and hilarious. The right to sleep all day and stay up all night."

The writer of this critical magazine article characterized Arundel as "a tyrant, whose aim is to make savages of his subjects by giving them the right to ignore ethical and moral laws established by mankind."

Feigning outrage, Arundel wrote to the magazine editor and to various Soviet leaders demanding an apology for the insulting language, and declaring Baldonian waters off-limits to the entire Russian fleet until such time as said apology was received. If need be, this ban would be enforced by the principality's navy, which consisted of Arundel's tuna-fishing boat, backed up, if necessary, by the might of the Armdale Yacht Club.

At some juncture in the exchange, it was pointed out to the Russians that the nation of Baldonia did not actually exist. Probably embarrassed at not being in on the joke, the Soviet Union failed to respond to Arundel's declaration, allowing him to claim for ever after that Baldonia had won a war with Russia.

In 1973, an aging Arundel shifted his interests to warmer southern waters and sold the island to the Nova Scotia Bird Society for the sum of one dollar; and so, after twenty-five years, the non-nation of Outer Baldonia ceased to exist.

The history of the rest of the Tusket Islands may not be quite as colourful, but is interesting nonetheless. Since the arrival of Europeans on these shores, many of the islands have been inhabited by fishermen seeking a closer proximity to the fishing grounds. During the 1800s, some of the larger islands, Like Big Tusket Island, built up proper communities with houses where people lived year-round. Stores, factories, and businesses were established to support the population scattered over the other islands.

Many of the smaller islands supported anywhere from one to several houses, which the islanders call "shanties", and a like number of wharves and out-buildings. Several of the islands featured lobster and tuna canneries, one island had a complete and well-stocked general store, and another boasted an elaborate stone lodge built to host wealthy sport tuna fishermen.

Gradually, as boats became motorized and the trip from the mainland ports to the fishing grounds grew less arduous, many of the smaller islands were deserted. By the mid-1900s, most of the remaining shanties were used only as summer homes or were occupied temporarily during the fishing season by fishers based out of Wedgeport and a few other nearby mainland villages.

One of these islands is Ellenwood Island. A long, narrow stretch of rock and sand, located on the western side of the group, it looks from the air a bit like an elongated and emaciated figure eight. It was once the site of a lobster cannery and several houses, but today only a few small buildings and a couple of wharves remain.

On December 20th, 1963, one of these buildings was being temporarily occupied by Lester Robbs and

"Little Barnard" Swim, two fishermen who were living out on the island for part of the week during lobster season.

They had been confined to their shanty for the last thirty-six hours by the winter storm lashing the area, but by mid-afternoon on Friday the weather had moderated enough for them to venture out with their shotguns in search of any ducks that may have taken shelter in the cove on the protected side of the island.

While approaching the northern end of the island, on the seaward side of the point, they came across the wreckage of a fishing boat.

Although the storm had let up quite a bit by now, it was still very windy, with rafts of broken sea-ice piling up along the windward shoreline. Due to the high tide, rough water, and surrounding ice, the two men were not able to reach the badly damaged boat, but as far as they could tell, there appeared to be no sign of life aboard.

They were able to get close enough to make out the name on the bow: *Ruth Lillian II.*

14: Breaking the news

It was a bit before five-thirty when the phone rang. Raymond had just finished his supper and was looking forward to a few minutes on the living-room couch before heading down the road to reopen the store for the evening.

He lifted the receiver and heard Elsie's voice. "Hello, Raymond? I tried to call you at both stores, but got no answer, so I thought I'd try you at home. I've got Constable Smith from the Digby RCMP on the line. He wants to talk to you."

Raymond had spoken to Smith earlier in the day. Since he was the registered owner of the *Ruth Lillian II*, the Constable had called him to get a description of the missing boat. The Digby Detachment had only just learned that morning of the missing boys by hearing about it on the Saint John news.

There was really not much action they could take at the moment, but Constable Smith had promised to pass along any relevant information that came their way. Raymond assumed that since he was now calling back, he must have some news.

"Hello, Constable Smith, what can I do for you?"

"I've got something for you. It's not good news, I'm afraid. Normally I'd prefer to deliver something like this in person, but since the Grand Passage ferry is not crossing today, it'll have to be over the phone. My apologies for that."

"No problem. I understand. This doesn't sound good. What did you find out?"

"Just a short time ago we received word from our Yarmouth Detachment that a boat has been found washed up on one of the Tusket Islands, near Wedgeport in Yarmouth County. They have not been able to get out to the island themselves to officially confirm this, but the local men that found the boat report that it is the *Ruth Lillian II.* I'm sorry to say that there has been no sign of any survivors at this time."

"Oh, my lord! That certainly is not the news I wanted to hear. That's too bad. Thank you for letting me know. I'll look after telling the family."

"I appreciate you doing that. I'll contact the Coast Guard about calling off their search, and I'll let you know if we receive any new relevant information."

The usual after-supper bustle and noise made by a house full of kids carried on around Raymond, but it all faded away from him as he sat alone with his thoughts for a few moments after the call ended.

This was the worst possible outcome, the one people had tried to avoid speaking out loud about, but for which everyone had been unconsciously preparing.

And now he had to go tell the families. It was going to be bad enough for Ace and Eileen to hear this, but for Ada and Percy it was going to be heart-breaking. The same thing all over again, a blow no parent should have to experience once in a lifetime, let alone twice.

His mind made one last grasp at a quickly fading ray of hope. Smith had said that no bodies had been found. Maybe there was still a chance. Maybe they were on the island somewhere. Maybe they had somehow survived.

At the end of his conversation with Smith, the Constable had passed on the contact number of the person who had reported the wreck. A quick call to Elsie, and Raymond found himself connected to Mrs. Simmons.

Within the first minute or two of their conversation, he felt his faint ray of hope dimming even further. By the time he had learned about the location and size of the island, the weather conditions, and the condition and position of the wrecked boat, whatever remained of that ray had been completely extinguished.

"I'll let you know if anything turns up," Mrs. Simmons promised before hanging up. "The men are going to try to get out to the boat this evening after the tide drops a bit. Right now they're searching along the shoreline. They've picked up a few bits and pieces that came off the boat, but that's all. There's rafts of ice piled up on the shore right now, so it's possible that anything under it might not be uncovered until it melts in the spring."

Ace was standing in what had lately become his usual spot, in front of the living room widow. Daylight was fading and the streetlight in front of his house had just blinked on when he noticed a blue pick-up truck pull into his yard. He shouted to Eileen and headed to the kitchen door.

The look on Raymond's face as he entered told him all he needed to know: he had news and it was not good. Ace's knees suddenly felt weak and he nearly collapsed onto one of the kitchen chairs, but instead willed himself to remain standing, gripping the back of the chair with both hands for support.

Eileen had entered the kitchen and was standing near the sink, twisting a dish towel in her hands. They both stared silently at Raymond, wanting, but at the same time not wanting, to hear what he had to say.

On the drive over to their house, Raymond had tried to formulate a plan for breaking the news. What should he say? How should he say it? What was the best way to tell them?

Whatever he had managed to come up with in the three-or-four-minute trip, it was now forgotten, and he just straight-forwardly reiterated the details as they had been told to him.

Before he was able to finish, Eileen ran from the room, holding the towel to her face to stifle her sobs. Ace slumped into the chair he had been leaning on; head bowed, hands clasped between his knees. He just sat and stared at the floor as Raymond finished delivering his unhappy news.

Ace sat motionless for a few moments after Raymond finished talking, then finally he looked up. "I'll tell Ada and Percy."

"Are you sure about that? I can come with you."

"No, that's okay. I'll do it."

"If the weather's fit for the ferry to cross tomorrow, I'll be going to Wedgeport to see if I can get out to have a look at the boat. If you want to come with me, meet me at the ferry first thing in the morning."

"Okay, yeah, I'll come with you. I'll be on the wharf."

After Raymond left, Ace spent the next few minutes sitting at the table. From the bedroom he could hear muffled sobs.

He forced himself to his feet, steadying himself for a few seconds by gripping the chair back with one hand and leaning on the table with the other before the room stopped spinning enough for him to take a step. He realized that the chair he had been sitting in was the one Donald usually used.

He considered going to Eileen, but thought better of it. There was nothing he could say that would help, and he knew she would rather be alone right now. Instead, he tried to shout, "I'm going to the lighthouse," in the direction of the bedroom, but all that came out was a strangled croak

Ace repeated his message, clearer this time, waited a few seconds for an answer, didn't get one, and headed out to his car.

15: Salvage rights

Saturday, December 21

Ace was just starting to feel the chill from the cold wind whipping in off the harbour when he saw Raymond pull up and park his truck behind the two other vehicles that were waiting in line for the ferry.

The ferry—the wooden scow and the modified fishing boat lashed to the side of it—had been brought back around from the lee side of the wharf and was now sitting out a ways from the ferry slip, in the protected corner created by the "L" shape of the wharf. Normally, by now it would be right in at the slip with its ramps down, ready and waiting to receive all comers as they arrived. But not today; today the leftover effects of the storm were still causing a heavy swell to roll into the dock, and the rise and fall it generated would have subjected the scow to a beating against the wharf and the concrete slip, had it sat there for any length of time.

Ace opened the truck door and jumped in, thankful to be in out of the cold.

"Been waiting long?" Raymond asked.

"No, not long. Just a few minutes."

They both looked up at the sound as the ferry engine roared to life, the indication that Captain Emerson Titus was about to move in to the slip. The stiff breeze quickly whipped away the plume of diesel smoke that shot out of the boat's exhaust stack.

They watched as the deckhand, Bun Dakin, stepped across the open water in the gap between the boat and the scow and then walked over to unhook the single line from the rusted iron rung of the wharf ladder that the ferrymen often used as a convenient temporary hitching point. The exhaust smoke thickened again as the sound of the diesel engine deepened and the ferry started to move in toward the slip.

The cars in front of Raymond's truck had already moved up a bit closer to the top of the slip in anticipation, so Raymond put the truck in gear and edged up, too.

He glanced over at Ace, who was staring stoically straight ahead. "How'd it go with Percy and Ada?"

"'Bout the way I expected: bad. They took it hard, real hard. Two sons lost now."

"I can't imagine what the four of you are going through."

"It's the not knowin' anything for sure that makes it hard to deal with. I guess at least after today we'll know what's what, one way or another."

Raymond followed the other cars down the slip and onto the scow. Another new arrival had timed it just right and drove out onto the wharf and down onto the scow behind him.

Often, the first ferry run of the day would be a busy one, usually a full load, especially in winter when the days were shorter. Since Brier Islanders had to cross two ferries to get to the mainland, and the ferries only operated during daylight hours, people who needed to conduct business off the island would leave first thing in the morning in order to have as much time as possible on the mainland and still be able to make it back before dark in time to catch the last ferry home.

Normally, Emerson would sit and wait until the ferry was fully loaded for this first run, or until he had decided he'd waited long enough: the ferry didn't run on a fixed schedule; it operated mostly according to need or at the captain's whim.

Today, because of the rough conditions in the dock, they were cutting their time spent sitting at the slip as short as possible: just get in, load, and get out. Bun started cranking the handle that manually raised the ramp back up as soon as the last vehicle rolled onto the scow.

As the ferry moved out along the wharf, the insistent honking of a horn could be heard.

In his rear-view mirror, Raymond could see a car sitting at the top of the slip, frantically flashing its headlights. Under calmer conditions, Emerson might have returned to pick up this late-comer, but today he'd have to wait for the next trip.

As the ferry left the protection of the wharf and started to buck out into the choppy waves of the open harbour, Raymond filled Ace in on what little new information he had. "According to the lady I spoke with last night, because of the way the tide runs down along that shore, things don't usually drift onto that island where the boat was found. She says the fishermen around there believe that the boat must have run up on that island while it was still under power."

"That would make sense. The wind comin' out of the south-west like it was, would have made it hard to get back home and driven them down toward Yarmouth. And at night and with the snow as thick as it was, it would have been easy for them to miss that harbour entrance. If you don't see that Cape Forchu light to guide you in, it's real easy to miss your chance and run right past. And with no radar on that boat, steamin' along blind, they coulda run right up on that island and then got swamped and washed out of the boat."

Ace paused a moment before continuing. "They've got to be around there somewhere close to the boat. I don't understand why they haven't found 'em yet."

"I guess we'll know more when we get there and see it for ourselves."

They lapsed into silence.

The ferry was half-way across the passage by now. The harbour was still full of waves, much smaller than during the height of the storm, but still large enough to occasionally cover the scow and its four vehicles with a drenching spray of salt water. For the rest of the crossing they sat in silence, interrupted only by the sound of the windshield wipers flicking back and forth.

Raymond had arranged with Mrs. Simmonds to have her husband take them out to Ellenwood Island in his lobster boat. It turned out that Brad Simmonds had been waiting out the storm in one of the buildings on the island, and had been one of the first on the scene after the wreck was discovered. He was in the group that had searched the shoreline, and had some of the recovered items stored in a shed on the island.

Ace hadn't had much to say beyond the initial greetings when they met on the wharf in Wedgeport.

He mostly kept to himself as they travelled out from the Tusket River and weaved their way among the islands. He left all the talking to Raymond, who was a little worried about how Ace was going to react upon seeing the wrecked boat.

But as soon as they reached the wharf on the lee side of Ellenwood Island, Ace was the first one off the boat, quickly helping with tying up, then waiting impatiently for the others.

As they walked across the island, he seemed unusually animated, full of nervous energy, asking questions and making observations about the weather, the water, the lay of the land.

He suddenly went quiet again as they crested a slight rise in the middle of the narrow island and the hull of the *Ruth Lillian II* came into view, perched on the rocky shoreline just above the high-water mark.

Even from a distance, the two men were shocked. A jagged hole in the starboard side of the hull, just about where the captain would have stood at the wheel, was clearly visible. The wheelhouse and its awning were completely gone. As they drew nearer, they realized that the entire cabin and most of the fore deck had also been torn away.

Making their way cautiously over the rocks and the ice floes that still surrounded the boat, they managed to get aboard.

What remained of the *Ruth Lillian II* was not much more than an empty shell, half-full of broken slabs of

Figure 8: What remained of the "Ruth Lillian II"

sea-ice. They could now see that another hole had been punched through on the opposite side of the hull, and that part of the stern had been smashed in. The floor boards had been torn out, and although the trawl tubs were nowhere to be seen, there were miles of trawl lines knotted up in the bilge, strung around the empty hull and draped over the sides. They trailed across the beach, twisted and snarled among the ice, and wrapped around the rocks.

Both radios were gone, the captain's chair and the steering wheel were torn out, the engine and hauling equipment were not there; even the reduction, a sort of marine transmission and probably the single most valuable item on the boat, was missing.

Working cautiously around the ice and the tangled trawl, they made their way to the bow.

There was not much left to see here. The sliding door into the cabin, and most of the framework it had been attached to, had been smashed out, leaving only a few splintered remnants to indicate where the bulkhead had been. What had been the cabin area was now almost completely gutted: bunks gone, table gone, lockers gone. Only the small cabin stove remained; bent and twisted, it was crushed high up into the bow, wedged tightly under the small piece of remaining deck as if thrust there by the hand of Neptune himself.

They noticed a partly disassembled microphone and a single rubber boot in the bottom of the boat.

"They must have been trying to fix that damn radio," said Ace. "The boot's not Donald's. Must be one of Gerald's."

As they made their way back aft, Ace pointed out a few haddock in the stern of the boat. "At least they caught some fish."

Climbing down off the boat, Ace noticed something, and, lying down on the ice, reached in under the curve of the hull and tugged at it a few times with no success. Raymond ducked down to see a green oilskin jacket pinned to the rocks by the hull.

"It looks like Donald's," Ace said.

The last change of tide had shifted some of the ice slabs that covered the beach, so Brad suggested they check along the shoreline in case something new had been uncovered. He was careful to not say out loud what was implied, that there could be a body under the ice.

Almost immediately, Ace identified a pole washed up on the beach near the boat, it had been attached to the wheelhouse to extend the radio antenna. It was generally agreed that this find gave more credence to the theory that the wheelhouse and awning were torn off after the boat had struck the island intact and under power.

"I'd really like to find out what happened to the equipment from the boat," Raymond said to Brad, "especially the reduction. It might give us some idea if they were still under power when they ran aground."

"I've got some of the stuff in my shed," Brad replied. "As soon as the tide dropped, there were several people here, salvaging everything they could before the boat was totally smashed up by the waves or washed out to sea again on the next high tide. Some items they gave to me to hold for you, some they took with them, but I know who's got what and I'm sure I can get it back. The only thing that might be a problem is the reduction. The guy who took it is well-known around here to be tight-fisted. I'm not sure he'll give it up without a fight."

"If we can't get it back, I'd like to at least have a look at it to see if it can tell us anything."

"I can take you over to see him. Like I said, he's kind of tight, and not the easiest guy to deal with, but we'll see what we can do."

Daniel Keizer was not only tight-fisted, as Brad had said, but tight-lipped as well. He was very reluctant to speak with Raymond and Ace, at first denying any knowledge of the reduction. "I don't know why you came to me, I don't have it, and whoever does have it has a salvage claim on it."

"Well, we're not concerned right now with who has a claim or not," Raymond replied. "We are just trying to figure out how that boat came to be on that island."

"How's the reduction going to help you with that?"

"If it was found still in gear, it means the boat was most likely under power when it ran aground. We were told you were one of the first to get on the boat and you helped get that piece of machinery out, so we want to know if you noticed if it was still in gear."

The realization that they were seeking information and not the immediate return of the equipment seemed to loosen Keizer's tongue slightly. "I wasn't the first one on the boat. That was Lester Robbs and Barnard Swim. They said the lever was all tangled up with trawl lines and there was a lot of ice sloshing back and forth in the boat. Either of those things could have shifted the lever. Plus, when we did get it out, the lever was just loose, flopping back and forth like it was broken, so I'm not sure it can tell you anything now."

"We'd still like to take a look at it for ourselves."

"Like I said, I don't have it, but I might know where it is. If the guy who has it was paid for the time he spent salvaging it, he might be willing to give it up."

"The Department of Fisheries has granted us the salvage rights to the boat," Raymond said, "so we'd like to get it back if we can. As far as who has a claim on what, and who deserves payment for what, we'll let the RCMP sort that out. They're conducting an investigation because of the loss of life, so they'll want to see anything that came off the boat and talk to anyone involved with removing equipment."

This information seemed to give Keizer pause. "I heard there might have been someone aboard, but didn't know for sure if it was true."

"Yes, two young men. My friend here is the father of the captain. It's not enough that the man has to deal with the loss of his own son as well as his sister's boy, now he's got to deal with people taking what little was left. The boat is owned by the bank, the insurance won't cover the full cost. We're here trying to find out what happened to those two boys, but also to salvage whatever we can to help cover some of the loss."

"I'm sorry to hear that," Keizer said, nodding in Ace's direction. He fell silent for a few moments, seemingly struggling with an inner conflict. Finally he addressed the two men. "I'll see that the reduction gets back to you. I'd just as soon not have any involvement with the police."

"I'll let them know that you helped us out," Raymond replied.

16: Investigation

January to May, 1964

Throughout the first few months of the new year, Constable Smith of the Digby RCMP continued to visit Brier Island to report on the process of their investigation. Unfortunately, given the circumstances, there had not been a lot to investigate at first.

Early on, before the boat was discovered on Ellenwood Island, Mounties had interviewed both families about the boys' fishing plans, and to get a physical and clothing description of each of them. As the owner, Raymond had to provide a description of the missing boat. This identifying information was forwarded to the RCMP detachments in Meteghan, Yarmouth, Barrington, and Shelburne, in case anything related to the investigation appeared on the shores in their district.

Franklin Gower of Westport was questioned on his brief interaction with the missing men while entering the passage, as were Llewelyn Theriault of East Ferry and Blair Titus of Digby, who had been fishing in the Brier Island area and were reported to have seen the *Ruth Lillian II* around the time of the storm.

These interviews with the fishermen added very little to the investigation, serving only to dispel rumours that the *Ruth Lillian II* had been sighted in the Brier Island area the day *after* the storm.

On January 9th, the Yarmouth Detachment made a patrol out to Ellenwood Island to investigate the wreck and interview local residents as to their involvement in finding and salvaging the boat. They were also asked, based on their knowledge of local tides and currents, for their opinions of how the boat came to be where it was found.

In one of his earlier reports, Smith noted that when he interviewed the families of the two boys on December 28, he learned that they felt there was no remaining hope, that that the boys could not have survived and were lost.

On January 15th, RCMP Superintendent L. J. C. Watson officially concurred with this assessment in a report to Nova Scotia's Deputy Attorney General, writing that "McDormand and Welch were swept overboard and consequently drowned while fishing in the Brier and Long Islands area." He went on to state, "There is the possibility that the bodies may be located after the spring breakup and the file will be held open until such a check can be made."

The final report Constable Smith submitted was dated April 30th and detailed the results of a conversation with Raymond, who had recently heard from Brad Simmonds and others. Now that the ice had melted, a group of locals had made a search of Ellenwood, as well as of several other near-by islands, but had recovered no bodies. Over the past four months however, several items from the *Ruth Lillian II*, including the awning and parts of the wheelhouse and cabin, had been discovered on some of these islands.

Given the location of the islands, and the type of items found on them, the conclusion drawn now by those most familiar with the intricacies of the Tusket Islands tides was that it was most likely that the awning and wheelhouse had been torn off and both boys swept overboard when the *Ruth Lillian II* was overtaken by a wave at some point before reaching the islands. Even if they were swamped later, closer to the island, given the tide and weather conditions at the time the boat came ashore, the likelihood was that both bodies would have been carried back out to sea by the receding tide.

Smith noted that, in light of this new information, Raymond had changed his opinion about the boat running onto the island under power. As well, after examining the equipment that had been salvaged from the boat, he found that the propeller had not been damaged. He now felt that the evidence proved that the boat's motor was not running when it came onto the beach, making it more than likely that the boat had undergone some catastrophic event at sea and had been disabled before being swept onto the island.

On May 5th, 1964, Superintendent Watson submitted a final report to the Deputy Attorney General in Halifax, which stated, "As no further action appears warranted at this time, we do not intend to pursue the matter further, however, should the bodies be located at a later date, you will be advised accordingly."

For all intents and purposes, this concluded the case as far as the RCMP were concerned. Unfortunately, it was not the end of the story for the families.

17: Aftermaths

For the police and the Coast Guard crews, even for the people of the Tusket Islands, the search for Donald and Gerald was over. The result was an unsatisfactory one, but for them, despite the unfortunate consequences of this voyage, life must go on.

For those more closely involved, the effects created by the loss of Donald and Gerald were much more long-lasting.

Ace McDormand carried on with the only life he had ever known, that of a fisherman. He continued going to sea, usually by himself, and often fishing out on the Southwest Ledge, the same area where his son had last fished.

It is said that bad things come in threes, and with his house burning down, his boat burning up, and the ultimate slap in the face by Lady Luck, the loss of his son—all within a period of about five years—Ace had certainly filled his quota with the worst kind of luck. But life was not quite done with kicking Ace McDormand around!

Just a few years after the loss of Donald and Gerald, Ace narrowly escaped with own his life when his boat exploded and burned while he was fueling up at D.B. Kenny's wharf. He was approaching seventy years of age by this time, and many in his situation would have recognized this as a clear sign from the powers that be that maybe it was time to retire.

Ace, on the other hand, took this as just one more challenge in his life. He had the nearly-destroyed hull of his boat hauled up into his front yard, where he proceeded to single-handedly transform it from the charred hulk it was back into a functioning fishing boat.

He re-launched his reconstructed boat and continued fishing for a few more years, until finally deciding on his own terms that it was time to retire.

He spent his last years going on road trips to the mainland in his old car, his dog a constant companion in the passenger seat beside him. The two could often be seen driving around the island, and it was not unusual to find them parked at Southern Point, Ace smoking one of his hand-rolled Player's and staring out to sea.

William Bernard "Ace" McDormand died in January of 1989 at the age of eighty-seven.

~

Eileen McDormand had always been a person who valued her privacy, and who kept her feelings to herself. After the events of December, 1963, she became even more solitary. As time passed, she practically became a recluse, rarely seen outside of her own house. She spent her last few years in a nursing home in the Annapolis Valley.

Lily Eileen (Sullivan) McDormand died in September of 1995 at the age of eighty.

~

Percy Welch did follow through on his plan to retire, doing so in November of 1964. However, his dream of travelling in his retirement years was not to be realized. In February of 1965, he was diagnosed with cancer and spent his next few months battling his deteriorating health, the effects of which were no doubt exacerbated by the toll the stress and pain of losing his two youngest sons took on him.

Percy Gordon Welch died in January, 1966 at the age of sixty-six.

~

Ada Welch persevered after the death of her husband. In the fall of 1966 she bought a small grocery store on Brier Island. After two years, the strain of running a business began to take a toll on her health, compelling her to sell the business and move to Saint John, New Brunswick, where she lived with her daughter Fannie. There she met and married Herman Flewelling in 1972.

In 1978 she once again became a widow. For much of this time, she maintained the Westport family home and returned there to spend her summers. In 1990 she suffered a stroke and spent her remaining years in a Saint John nursing home.

Ada Marguerite (McDormand) Welch died In August of 1998, one week after her birthday, at the age of 90.

~

Berton Welch gave up the fishing life and sold his boat shortly after the loss of Donald and Gerald. He thereafter made his living by working at jobs that mostly kept him off the water. In 1975, his son, Gordon, was killed in a car accident. A few months later Berton suffered a heart attack.

Berton Welch died in November of 1977.

~

Carolyn Welch never got a chance to go in search of the new life that she and Gerald had hoped to find. She remarried and lived out the rest of her life on Brier Island.

Carolyn Margaret (Howard, Welch) Frost died in April of 2012.

~

Raymond Robicheau shut down his fish business in the 1970s due to the decline in the fisheries, and closed the little store not long after. He then concentrated on growing and expanding business at his remaining store. In February of 1976 the building that housed this store was totally destroyed by a tidal wave in the Groundhog Day Storm that devastated much of southwestern Nova Scotia.

With the help of friends and family, and the support of many of his customers, Raymond managed to recover and build back better than ever, eventually having the only surviving store on the island out of five that had been in operation at the beginning of the 1960s.

At the time of this writing, Raymond Eugene Robicheau is looking forward to celebrating his one hundredth birthday in June of 2023.

18: The search for David

For the rest of her life, right up until the day she died, Ada Welch lived with the hope and belief that her second-oldest son was still alive somewhere and that he would someday return to her. Although she never doubted that Gerald and Donald were dead, when it came to David, she often spoke to her family of the unexplained, but persistent feeling she had: "He's not gone. He is out there somewhere, but where?"

David Welch's story started out similarly in many ways to that of his brother, and it appeared to many that it had a similarly sad ending; but for those who cared the most about him, there was reason to believe that his story had not reached its end at all, that there may yet be a more hopeful conclusion.

After living and working briefly in Saint John and finding that city life was not for him, David had made a deliberate decision—against the advice of both his parents and his fisherman brother, Berton—to buy his own boat and take up a life of fishing. In July of

1959, at the age of nineteen, he became the proud owner and captain of the *Elaine D*, a forty-two foot, twenty-year-old Cape Islander.

David's first few months as captain of his own vessel were quite eventful; and for his parents, quite worrisome.

His first mishap took place within weeks of acquiring his new boat. This was the aforementioned exhaust leak that rendered both Gerald and David unconscious as they were crossing the bay. During this time, David fell against the hot exhaust pipe and received a severe burn to his thigh, leaving a noticeable scar.

On that occasion their uncle Ace and cousin Donald rescued the boys. A month later, David had the opportunity to return the favour when he pulled Donald off of Ace's burning boat.

A few weeks after this, David was reported missing when he failed to show up as expected in Westport. After leaving Grand Manan, he had been caught at sea by unexpected high winds, rough seas, and thick fog. With only a faulty compass to help him navigate, he had no idea where he was.

Running blind in extremely bad weather, he managed to keep the *Elaine D* afloat, and after several hours, eventually beached her safely on Black Beach in Lorneville, on the New Brunswick side of the Bay of Fundy.

On the night of October 23rd, only four months after taking ownership of the *Elaine D*, David once again left Whitehead Harbour, and this time vanished in the Bay of Fundy somewhere between Grand Manan and Brier Island.

For a second time, he was reported as missing, and on the 25th was listed as "Lost and Presumed Drowned". No body was ever found.

Even with all the unknown circumstances attached to Donald and Gerald's situation, the McDormand and Welch families were eventually able to accept their loss. But when it came to David, in the minds of Ada and Percy the fate of their second-oldest son was not as clear-cut. As far as they were concerned, there could be many plausible answers to what they felt were the unanswered questions surrounding Davis's disappearance.

To them, the central question was, "What happened to David?"

On the night that David disappeared, the weather was relatively calm, so the crossing of the bay should have been an easy one, and one that David was thoroughly familiar with, having made the trip many times before.

What had transpired out on the water that night? What series of events could have removed David from his vessel but left it running and able to return almost exactly to the place from which it had started?

One simple possibility, and the one many people found most likely, was that David somehow fell overboard. The boat was loaded to the gunwales with herring, a particularly oily fish. A greasy deck would make any climbing or moving around on the boat even more risky than usual.

To get to the bow or stern area, David would have had to walk along the narrow washboard on the outside of the boat. It would only take a slip of the foot, a sudden jolt from an unexpected wave, or a missed hand-hold to throw him off balance, and he would have been in the water with no chance of rescue. It's possible that something as simple as attempting to retrieve a dragging rope from the stern or bow had led to an unfortunate slip.

Like many fishermen at the time, David could not swim. But even if he could, he was alone on the voyage and would have only been able to watch in despair as his boat sailed away without him.

Another theory, derived from an examination of the damage to one side of the *Elaine D.* that did not seem likely to have been caused by the boat running aground, was that she had been struck by another, larger vessel. The fact that David's running lights were not working when he left Whitehead Harbour to cross the bay at night would seem to lend a bit more credence to this theory. The collision could have spun the smaller boat around, heading her back in the direction of Grand Manan; and, maybe catching David unawares and throwing him overboard on impact.

Over time, the plausibility of this scenario was reinforced when a rumour circulated that a foreign ship, possibly fishing illegally in the area, was seen leaving the Bay of Fundy on that same night, raising the possibility that an injured or unconscious David had been rescued by the very ship that had run him down. Most likely not wanting the trouble of being examined too closely, or the expense of being involved in an accident investigation in foreign waters, the ship then would have continued on its way.

This theory gained further credence when someone connected to the RCMP suggested to the family that a Russian ship may have been involved, saying that such a ship might well stop to pick up a survivor at sea, but would not return to port. The usual practice in these cases was that the person would be cared for and kept on board as a crew member. The next destination would most likely be a Russian port.

This story was the one that the Welch family chose to cling to. They came to believe that there was a reasonable and realistic possibility that David had survived, and, over time, it appeared that there may be some actual evidence to justify and bolster Ada's strongly-held belief in her son's survival.

The first indication that there may be reason for hope came in the early 1960s, when Carl Swift, a resident of Westport, reported that he had noticed a young man on the Halifax waterfront who bore a striking resemblance to David. When he called out David's name, the man ducked down one of the side streets and disappeared.

Then, in February of 1966, David's sister, Freda, was finishing up her shopping in a Saint John Kmart. When she went to look for her husband, she found him watching three Russian sailors who were standing at the music counter. One of the group was a very familiar-looking young man, dressed differently from the other two, who seemed to be translating for his comrades. Upon realizing they were being watched, the three whispered among themselves and then left the store.

Three days later, Freda related this story to her sister Fannie, impressing on her the distinct resemblance this sailor bore to their brother. Fannie contacted the Port Authority and found that there had been a Russian cargo ship in port for the past several days. The crew member list for this ship contained only one non-Russian-sounding name, David Wilson, or Wilcox—the last name was not entirely legible.

Fannie asked permission to board the ship and speak with this crewman, but discovered that it had already left port, six hours ahead of schedule.

For the next twenty-seven years there were no more sightings or any other evidence to bolster the belief that David was still alive.

Then, starting in March of 1993, Juanita, who had been a good friend of David's and was the last one to see him before he left Whitehead Harbour,, got a series of mysterious phone calls.

The male caller would ask, "Is that you, Nita?"

When she replied, "Yes, this is Nita," the line would disconnect.

This happened several times, with the last call coming in May of the same year.

Juanita informed Fannie of these calls, and when she asked why Juanita thought the phone calls were significant, she replied, "Because the only one that ever called me Nita was David."

Fannie also learned from 'Juanita' that David's boat, which the family had given permission to have towed off the rocks and sunk out in the bay, had actually floated into Whitehead Harbour, where it came to rest on the beach right in front of her house. Every day for years, she had looked out on the wreck of the *Elaine D* until she finally deemed it too much of a hazard for her kids to play on, and had it burned.

About a month after the last phone call was made, Fannie was watching a report on ATV News about the arrival of two Russian warships in Halifax Harbour. As the camera panned over the crew, she was shocked to realize that one of the men looked very familiar to her brother. The next morning she contacted the ATV affiliate in Saint John and arranged to review the news clip.

After watching the very brief shot of the crewman in question, she contacted the Halifax office of ATV, and she and her husband left the next day to see the complete, unedited tape.

Upon getting a better look at the crewman, they decided that, although the resemblance was remarkable, he was much too young to be David. In fact, he looked young enough to be David's son.

By chance, the ship was holding a visitors' day the next day, so Fannie and Cyril took advantage of the opportunity to get an in-person look. Observing at first from a distance, Fannie could see that the young man seemed to have many of the postures and mannerisms of her brother. She overheard him speaking to visitors in very good English, and when she asked for a picture with him, he understood her completely and happily complied.

The young man told her that his name was Yousif, and he appeared happy to chat with her and answer her questions; but when she asked him if it was possible that his father was Canadian, he replied in perfect English that he could not understand the question.

The opportunity to speak with Yousif ended at this point, and this phase of Fannie's investigation came to an end.

Since her visit to the Russian ship had not really provided any answers, only more questions, and she was feeling frustrated with the lack of results this line of inquiry had provided, Fannie decided to try a different approach. Following up on the possible Russian connection, she contacted the Red Cross in Moscow, inquiring as to the possibility of tracking foreign nationals in the Russian bureaucracy.

Eight months later she got a reply to the effect that, although there were many 'Unidentifiables' in the USSR—including people in prison camps—due to Cold War restrictions at the time, access to their records by outside agencies was not allowed.

Fannie also made inquiries closer to home. She searched through the records of several agencies, including the Department of Fisheries, the Coast Guard, and the RCMP, and the only government file on David Welch that could be uncovered was his death certificate, issued less than a month after his disappearance, with an incorrect date of death and with no proof of that death, declaring him as "Lost and presumed drowned."

Except for this single document, despite David having been twice reported missing, there was no other record of a search or investigation. It almost seemed that, except for the death certificate, David Welch had never officially existed.

It appeared that Fannie's search had reached another dead end.

19: Persistent hints

Throughout the 1980s and into the 1990s, the popular "Day in the Life" series of books was published. Each year, the editor of this book would pick a different country to feature, and arranged for photographers to spread out through the towns, cities, and countryside on a certain day to record, through pictures and stories, events that might give the reader a twenty-four-hour window into one typical day in the life of the residents of that country.

On September 9th, 1993, while visiting her daughter, Fannie happened to leaf through a copy of 1987's *A Day in the Life of the Soviet Union.* On page 138 she came across a picture of a prisoner in Vladimir Prison, one of the infamous Soviet Gulags. He was standing beside a machine at a workbench, and he looked an awful lot like a younger version of her father.

Eddie Adams, a Pulitzer Prize-winning freelance photographer based out of New York, had taken the picture. Fannie managed to track down Adams, and asked him what he could tell her about that day and that photo. He recalled that while he was setting up his equipment out in the yard, one of the prisoners approached him and asked in fluent English if that was a Nikon camera, Adams thought that was odd because, at that time, Nikon cameras were rare and not well known in Russia.

Since he had been allotted only a very short time to set up and take his pictures, Adams was distracted and did not pay close attention to the appearance of the prisoner, so could not say for sure if he was the same one who appeared in the book. He did recall that the man appeared to be about fifty years of age, which would have been David's age at the time, and that he had very distinct blue eyes, like David.

Adams said he had a general impression that the man in the yard seemed to be out of place among the other prisoners, and recalled that the reason his editor later chose to print the picture of the prisoner by the bench, out of the hundreds of pictures Adams had taken that day, was that he said he had the feeling that this person "did not belong in that environment".

Gulags were, in part, political prisons; a person could be sent there for speaking out against the government, expressing anti-communist sentiments, not producing the correct identification papers upon demand, or for as little as tossing a cigarette butt into the street. It's possible that someone brought into the country without proper identification, and unfamiliar with its laws and customs, could very well have ended up in a gulag for a time.

Before hanging up the phone, Adams happened to mention that the man who asked about the camera had been standing in front of a newly-painted building.

Fannie asked him if the building had been painted salmon pink with white trim and a green door.

He replied, "Yes, it was. How did you know?"

"Because," Fannie replied, "those were the colours David painted the family home right before he disappeared."

Fannie made another attempt to obtain information on foreign prisoners in Russia, specifically those in Vladimir Prison, but the inquiry proved fruitless. Once again, her investigation had stalled.

In April of 1994, on a visit to Grand Manan Island, Fannie and Cyril discovered that, shortly after Juanita had stopped getting those mysterious phone calls, another friend of David's had started receiving calls by ship-to-shore radio. The caller would ask to speak to 'Maggie', and when she replied, the connection—as with the phone calls—would be dropped.

Also, as with the phone calls, the only person who

had ever called this lady 'Maggie' was David.

Some time in the late 1990s, Fannie was listening to a call-in show on Saint John radio station CFBC. The subject up for discussion was "Living in Canada: how does it compare to other countries?" A caller was commenting about how fortunate Canadians are, compared to some of the countries he had lived in, and Fannie realized that he had a very familiar voice.

She contacted the host of the show, and found that the caller had given his name as David Vladimir, and that the call had come from somewhere in the general area of Yarmouth, Nova Scotia.

The Yarmouth RCMP knew of no one by that name in the vicinity and suspected that the call may have come from a crew member one one of the foreign fishing vessels that had been docked in Shelburne at the time.

Noting the connection between the surname of Vladimir and her earlier investigation of Vladimir Prison, Fannie spent the next few years trying to track down David Vladimir. She found a possible connection to a prisoner who had been released from Vladimir Prison and then appeared to show up later working in a factory in Switzerland. Eventually, she was able to learn that a retired gentleman of that name lived in a small town near Lake Geneva in

Switzerland, but she had no luck getting in direct contact with him.

By chance, in 1997, Westport resident Arden Derby befriended a visitor to the island who was from Switzerland and lived not too far from where David Vladimir was believed to reside. He and Arden kept in touch by email, and, after talking with Fannie, Arden asked his friend if he would mind looking up Vladimir and asking him a few questions.

Privacy laws are very strict in Switzerland, and it would be considered very rude to approach a stranger unsolicited and ask personal questions. Arden's friend gave the request some serious thought. In fact, it would be four years later when he agreed to visit David Vladimir.

Armed with a list of questions from Fannie, he made the visit and later reported back.

The visit had not been productive. Although he agreed to the visit, Vladimir was evasive, gave contradictory answers to some of the questions, and refused to answer others. Arden's friend observed that, in his opinion, Vladimir was not a native Swiss, and not very forthcoming.

From the answers she was able to get, and the few details Vladimir revealed about himself, Fannie concluded that, once again, she had reached a dead end.

Although Fannie continued to believe in the possibility of David's survival, and for the rest of her life would keep her mind open to any further indications of his existence, this was the end of her active investigations. During the years of her search, and continuing on into the ensuing years, she would get information that seemed to indicate that her brother might still be alive. Unfortunately, while this information may have encouraged her to keep looking, and helped to keep her belief alive, it was not the type of information she could easily investigate.

In 1982, Fannie and a friend visited a psychic on a whim to have their tea leaves read. The friend was told about her future. Fannie was told about her past, including two accidents involving brothers. She was informed that the person in the second accident was gone, but the one in the first accident was still alive.

In 1993, just as she was planning her trip to Halifax to tour the Russian warships in search of Yousif, Fannie and her daughter revisited the same psychic, this time for a Tarot card reading. Her daughter was told about her future. Fannie was told, "Get going, search for someone, brother perhaps, connection may be broken, I see ships and water."

In 2000 Fannie and a friend visited a different psychic. Her friend was told about her future. Fannie was told, "The person you are looking for is alive."

Upon leaving, Fannie noticed an advertisement for 'Missing Person Readings' and booked an appointment. At this reading Fannie was told, "Yes, this person is alive."

The psychic described details of the accident, rescue, and the foreign ships lying offshore, then said, "This person is no longer in the same country," and suggested that Fannie concentrate her search on Switzerland.

In 2001, Fannie's niece, Janet, was having coffee with a friend in Thunder Bay, Ontario, when a picture that Fannie had taken at one of her readings fell out of Janet's purse.

Her friend, a non-practising psychic, picked it up and made several observations:

> "This person is still alive and was rescued by men speaking a foreign language."
>
> "There was a large boat offshore. The name was foreign, but cannot be made out."
>
> "Switzerland is a place to search for this person."

The friend also went into David's past, accurately describing him as he was when a little boy, including his favourite toy.

Except for the advice to search in Switzerland,

Fannie received very little actual information that she could follow up on from these sessions with psychics, but it did seem to strengthen her belief that she was on the right track and that her brother could yet be found, and it bolstered her faith in her mother's confident insistence that David was still alive.

20: What may have happened

So, what *did* happen to David, and to Gerald and Donald? The truth is that we don't know; we will never know. All we can do is speculate.

In David's case, in my personal opinion, the most likely answer is the simplest one. It's a story that I'm sure is as old as the invention of the boat, and has likely been told since man first decided to go out on the water unaccompanied: he slipped and fell overboard. David couldn't swim and the boat, still under power, would have sailed off without him, leaving him with no chance of survival.

But then again, Ada's strongly-held belief, despite the complete lack of evidence at the time, that David was still alive, also has to be taken into consideration. A mother's intuition cannot be easily dismissed.

One could say this feeling of hers was based on nothing more than a desperate hope. There were no facts, no supporting evidence; only, understandably, a grieving mother's refusal to accept the sudden loss of her child.

But over the years, evidence seemed to material-ize in the most surprising ways. Little clues here and there began to trickle in, there were mysterious calls in the night, unexpected sightings, messages from another realm. Although obscure, and few and far between, these faint tracks formed a trail that Fan-nie, the loving sister and daughter, diligently fol-lowed.

Despite repeatedly being led down blind alleys and finding herself facing yet another dead end, or blocked by bureaucracy or nonsensical rules and regulations, she spent a good part of her life search-ing; and even when it seemed the trail had run out, she never gave up on the hope that one day she would find out what had happened to David.

The one lead that Fannie spent most of her time on, the one that seemed the strongest and most promising, was the possibility that David had been picked up by a Russian ship and transported to a life in the Soviet Union. This was not an entirely unlikely scenario; such things had been known to happen be-fore and have happened since.

But why would he not eventually return home, or at least let someone know he was alive? Amnesia from a blow to the head when his boat was run down is one suggestion; but then, how would he re-member names and phone numbers so he could make those mysterious calls?

The mystery that Fannie tried her best to unravel still exists. Maybe someday someone, somewhere, will reveal the answers—if there are answers—that Fannie searched so long to find.

The story of Donald and Gerald has its own air of mystery. We know the beginning chapters of the story and the sad ending, but the middle will forever remain closed to us. We are left to write our own middle story.

Based on the combined knowledge of the fishermen of Brier Island and those of the Tusket Island group, we can make an educated guess at the events that take place within those few closed pages:

Dawn was just starting to break. Donald was at the wheel, and Gerald was in the cabin, pulling on his oilskins, preparing to head back outside to see if he could help Donald spot the entrance to Yarmouth Harbour.

A mile behind them, a wave was raging on, rolling in from deeper water, approaching the shallower water that surrounds the Tusket Islands.

Donald was starting to think that maybe he had missed Yarmouth altogether. Through the snow and the ice-covered wheelhouse windows, he hadn't been able to catch any sight at all of the Cape Forchu light.

Maybe now that it was beginning to come daylight, he could catch a glimpse of the shoreline and figure out where they were. They must be close, but even if they had already passed Yarmouth, there were other places along here where they should be able to find shelter.

The wave drew closer now, rolling over everything in its path, rising and falling, feeding voraciously off the wind and the now-shallowing bottom. It had become a looming wall of green water, building constantly to a new height, a new intensity, a new hunger.

Gerald had struggled back into his oilskin pants with their over-the-shoulder straps, then into his heavy coat. He shoved his feet back into his boots, and was just about to open the cabin door when he noticed that, in the confined space of the small cabin, he had inadvertently knocked the microphone he had been intending to repair off the table. He bent to pick it up.

The wave was moving faster now, racing along on the shallower bottom. Just ahead, like a puny leaf in a raging torrent, floated the Ruth Lillian II.

Donald was looking through a small clear spot in one of the port-side windows, his eyes fixed intently on the faint shape of what he was hoping was a distant shoreline. He paid no attention when the stern of the boat began to rise—after all, it had done that hundreds of times this night.

The stern continued to rise. Suddenly, Donald's concentration on the distant shore was broken by the overwhelming sense of a dark and ominous presence. He turned instinctively towards the stern.

It started to fall, then collapsed with a vengeance. The floodgates were released. Thousands of tons of emerald-green water crashed in over the stern, rushing forward, flooding, foaming, tearing and destroying, exploding everything in its path.

Gerald had just placed the microphone back on the table when he thought he heard Donald yell. He reached out to slide open the cabin door when there was a tremendous roar and the door suddenly exploded in toward him.

The wave, having done its worst, spat out the broken remnants of the puny obstacle that had been in its path and continued unconcernedly on its way.

The shattered hull of the *Ruth Lillian II,* crippled, stripped of its awning, its wheelhouse and its cabin, driven on by the relentless wind and waves, continued alone, empty now, drifting toward Ellenwood Island.

21: A story of two families

This story does not come to a satisfactory conclusion. Things are not wrapped up in a neat little bow. There is no joyous reunion at the end of the tale, no happy home-coming where the long-lost son returns to the loving bosom of his family.

And this is not simply the story of Ace and Eileen, who lost their only son and responded in very different ways—he by continuing to do what was familiar to him, the only thing he had ever known, going to work out on the water; she by receding even further into her own safe space.

Nor is it just the story of Percy and Ada, who were somehow able to come to terms with the fact that they would never again see their youngest son, Gerald, but clung fiercely to the hope that they might be able to find David. Ada lived out the rest of her life believing in her unexplained feeling that her son still existed somewhere in the world and that all that was needed was for him to be found.

And it is not just the story of Fannie, a dutiful

daughter and faithful sister who started out on a search, mostly to support and comfort her mother, and eventually came to share her mother's belief that her brother could be found and brought home again. Fannie spent more than sixty years of her life hunting for David, following obscure clues to his whereabouts, and seeking meaning in otherworldly references to his continued existence.

Although they obviously were the most affected, this story involved and touched more than just the immediate families. I was just about to turn eleven years old when David disappeared, and had just entered my fifteenth year when Donald and Gerald were lost. These were people I knew; Donald and my uncle Benny were good friends.

My father was involved in this, both financially and emotionally. I remember Ace, looking lost and hopeless, coming to talk to my father. I remember Gerald's new bride, Carolyn, distraught and being protected and comforted in her grief by friends and family. I remember the rough old fishermen on the store bench, showing uncharacteristic kindness to a grieving father.

The memory of these two tragedies, and people's reactions to them, stayed with me the rest of my life. I always thought that these stories should be told, that the memories of these young men should not be lost.

Over the years, I came to realize that this was not just a story of two families. It was a story that represented all who had suffered a similar fate, a story that has been repeated, in various forms, many times over the centuries, in many houses on these two islands. It is the story of the dangerous reality that those who make their living on the sea—and those at home who watch and wait for those who have gone to sea—have to live with every day.

Among the earliest records of the Long and Brier Island area, the name of James McIntyre can be found. He was one of a group of United Empire Loyalist grantees who were drowned in the Bay of Fundy in 1790 while on their way to take up land grants on the islands as reward for their loyalty to the Crown during the American Revolutionary War. They are among the earliest recorded victims on what was to become a long list of island residents lost to the sea since then.

One of the better-known names on the list is that of Brier Island's most famous resident, Joshua Slocum. Slocum was the first documented person to sail solo around the world. Leaving from Sambro, Nova Scotia in July of 1895 in his thirty-nine-foot sloop *Spray*, he arrived at Newport, Rhode Island three years later, in July of 1898.

Slocum wrote a book about his adventure, *Sailing Alone Around the World*, that has become a bible for solo sailors and is in print to this day. He talked of undertaking a second circumnavigation, and, in November of 1909, set out in the *Spray* from Vineyard Haven, Massachusetts, bound for the West Indies.

As David Welch would do almost exactly fifty years later, Slocum, alone on his boat, sailed out into that ocean wilderness and disappeared without a trace. In 1924 he was declared legally dead.

The rest of the names on that long list may not be as well-known to the average person; but to the mothers and fathers, to the wives and husbands, to the brothers and sisters, they are all equally important.

In 1967, Canada's Centennial Year, the town of Digby erected a monument on their waterfront to honour the memory of one hundred Digby County fishermen who have lost their lives at sea. On top of the memorial sits a large brass bell that was once installed at Northern Point to warn mariners of the shoals around Brier Island. Around the base of the monument are engraved the hundred names. For many of those listed here, their names on this monument are all that remains of their stories, as those who knew and loved them are long gone.

Among those listed are David Welch, Gerald Welch, and Donald McDormand.

Fannie Francis (Welch) Urquhart passed away on February 22, 2023 at the age of 88, the last member of her immediate family. Right up to the end of her life she kept the memory of her family's tragedy alive, still hoping for the big break that would help her find her brother. Just weeks before her passing, she referred to the possibility that David, an old man now, could still be alive somewhere, maybe with a family of his own, and children and grandchildren whom she would never get to know.

It is the policy of the Royal Canadian Mounted Police to keep unresolved missing-person files open until the person in question would have reached the age of one hundred and ten.

David Welch's file will be closed in 2050.

Donald McDormand's file will be closed in 2051.

Gerald Welch's file will be closed in 2052.

For a comprehensive list of
Long and Brier Island residents lost at sea,
visit John Thurber's *Lost at Sea List*:

https://sites.rootsweb.com/~nsdigby/lists/lost-sea.htm

Figure 9: The memorial in Digby

A Wilderness of Water

Ben Robicheau

Acknowledgements

The idea for this book had been lying dormant in the back of my mind for nearly sixty years. A chance meeting with Fannie Welch-Urquhart in my sister's sun-porch a few years ago stirred it back to life. I would like to thank Fannie for showing me that there was indeed a story there, and for all the long-distance question and answer sessions, your sharing of memories, and provision of official documents. I'm sorry, Fannie, that you didn't get to see the project complete.

I would like to thank Debbie Cusack, Fannie's daughter, for her help in finding documents and information and in arranging communication with her mother.

Thanks to Jan Morton-Maynard, Fannie's niece, who polled the family and provided me with permission to tell their story, and who also clarified some family details.

Thanks to Clayton Titus for help with technical aspects and with his sharing of personal memories.

Thanks also to Arden Derby for his memories of his involvement in the search for David.

I would like to thank my wife Randi, and my children, Sarah and Michael for their encouragement, my friend Jim Prime for showing me how it's done, and setting a high bar for me to strive for, and my grandchildren, Felix, Charlie, and Lyla, for demonstrating to me the excitement of learning new things, no matter your age.

Thanks also to Rebekah Wetmore for the cover design, and to Andrew Wetmore, who stops the sentences from running on, and keeps the participles in the past.

About the author

Ben Robicheau is a retired Jack-of-all-trades now living in Hamilton, Ontario. For several years he contributed regularly to *Passages,* the monthly newsletter of Long and Brier Islands, where he grew up. This column consisted of personal childhood reminiscences, adventures, and historical events unique to growing up on those islands at the end of Digby Neck.

His next contribution to *Passages* was a collaboration with fellow islander and author of over twenty books, Jim Prime. *Gurrey and Grime of The Digby Neck and Island Fish-Gutting Service and Detective Agency* was a monthly series of fictional stories relating the wildly-improbable adventures of a pair of aged island residents.

In 2017 Ben and Jim again joined forces and wrote a play, "Funeral Sandwiches", based on the Gurrey and Grime characters, that was chosen as 'The People's Choice' at the annual King's Shorts Ten-Minute Play festival at King's Theatre in Annapolis Royal

In 2020, Ben and Jim compiled these stories into a book for Moose House Publications, *Fish and Dicks: Case files from the Digby Neck & Islands Fish-Gutting Service & Detective Agency.*

The following year, Ben wrote and Moose House published *Two Ferries Out: growing up on Brier Island*, a collection of the previous *Passages* stories and some added material. This became the best-selling book for 2021 for Moose House.

There is a rumour that, if the weather holds fair, Prime and Robicheau will be bringing out a sequel to *Fish and Dicks* in the near future.